THE
JOB FINDER'S
BOOK

THE
JOB FINDER'S
BOOK

The Daily Telegraph
Guide

Fifth Edition

RUTH SANDYS
ALEXA STACE

**Kogan
Page**

First published in 1978
Fourth edition 1983, reprinted 1984
Fifth edition 1986
Published by Kogan Page Ltd
120 Pentonville Road, London N1 9JN

British Library Cataloguing in Publication Data

Sandys, Ruth
    The job finder's book: The Daily
    Telegraph guide.
    1. Job hunting
    I. Title   II. Stace, Alexa
    650.1'4   HF5382.7

    ISBN 1-85091-125-8

Printed and bound in Great Britain by
Guernsey Press, Guernsey, Channel Islands

CONTENTS

INTRODUCTION

This book is a step-by-step guide to the mechanics of finding a job. It is aimed at all young job-hunters, particularly those who leave school at CSE/O level standard. Some may have been out in the job market for some time, while others will just have left school. But whatever the age, the problems are the same when it comes to looking for a job.

In the face of the competition caused by severe job shortages in many parts of the country it is more than ever necessary to pay close attention to every step of the job-finding process. In this book we examine all those steps in detail from initial self-examination through required qualifications to letters of application and preparation for interview.

HOW TO USE THIS BOOK

☐ Start by deciding what sort of job you are looking for. Analyse yourself by going through the job types and seeing which one you fit into (Chapter 1).

☐ Having decided which job type you belong to, turn to the Job Guide (Chapter 2) and find out more about the jobs suggested for your type. If your entry qualifications are not good enough, look at Chapters 3 and 8 where the opportunities to improve your skills and qualifications are spelled out.

☐ Next consider how you can improve your chances through further education and training. You can improve your qualifications so as to get the job you want, or you can go in at a lower level and train on the job. We also tell you about apprenticeships (Chapter 3).

☐ Now you know what you are looking for, and have checked the qualifications necessary, you can start the search. We tell you where to look for job advertisements, who to ask for help, and how to organise yourself so that your hunt will be more efficient (Chapter 4).

☐ Once you start applying, we show you how to write effective letters of application, how to fill in application forms, how to draw up your curriculum vitae (cv) and how to apply by phone (Chapter 5).

☐ When you get an interview, we tell you how to sell yourself to the interviewer, how the interview is planned so that you will know what to expect, key questions to be prepared for and, at the end, key questions you ought to ask. We also tell you how to cope with a telephone interview (Chapter 6).

☐ When you are offered a job, we show you how to write the letter of acceptance (or refusal). We give you advice about the contract of employment, about first starting your job, and we give you a checklist of things you should find out about your job (Chapter 7).

☐ If you *still* have not found a job by now, we tell you what plan of action to follow and give information about the Government training schemes (YTS and Job Training Scheme) for young people having trouble finding jobs (Chapter 8).

Chapter 1

WHAT KIND OF JOB ?

To find a job, you first have to know what you are looking for and be clear about what you have to offer. You may be one of the lucky ones who have known from the age of five that you want to be a nurse or a car mechanic or whatever, but lots of people have only the haziest idea of what they would like to do — and that makes job-hunting a lot harder.

Your first priority then is to sort yourself out. No one can really help you in the job-hunt until *you* know what you are looking for.

You must ask yourself: What do I *want* to do? What *can* I do? Where will I fit in? What do I have to offer an employer?

There are literally hundreds of different jobs to choose from. You could try to find out about them all, trying to narrow down the choice, or you can begin from the other end by looking at yourself.

What sort of person are you?

We have listed below the main job types, and you must decide which one you fit into best. But first, you must get used to the idea of looking at yourself objectively and being realistic about your good and bad points.

(a) PHYSICALLY

For a lot of jobs your physique is irrelevant — cashiers, for instance, come in all shapes, sizes and states of fitness. But there is no point deciding to be a deep-sea diver if you are a seven-stone weakling. Equally, if you are a rugged outdoors type who was always better at football than maths, you might be miserable stuck in an office all day. But if you really have set your heart on a particular career, don't let physical disability put you off. If you want to join the police force, and you happen to be large and tough, it is a help — but they also want all the brains they can attract. So if your O levels are more impressive than your muscles, you will find that you are just as welcome.

If physical disability *is* a problem, it is well worth talking it over with a careers adviser, who may be able to suggest a compromise solution. If you are rejected as a pilot, for example, you might well find a job working as a flight engineer or in the control tower. The sort of jobs where a good physique is essential are:

☐ diving
☐ farming
☐ building trade
☐ Merchant Navy
☐ forestry and horticulture
☐ nursing
☐ Armed Forces
☐ working with animals.

(b) ACADEMICALLY

What sort of school record do you have? Are you a good all-rounder or outstanding at one or two subjects and mediocre at the rest? Or is your record pretty erratic, up and down according to who your teacher was that year? Try to sort out the long-term pattern. Are your 'good' subjects really your best ones, or the ones you most enjoy? Could you be better at your 'weak' subjects if it really mattered? Do you find it easier to understand and absorb a subject once its practical applications have been explained to you?

(c) INTERESTS

If you are the sort of person whose hobbies or outside interests seem to change every six months or so, depending on the latest fashion, then they are unlikely to provide a pointer towards a career. Again, look at the long-term pattern. Try writing down all your hobbies for the last three years or so, and see if there is any consistent thread. For example, if you have worked your way through Scouts, youth clubs, debating societies, drama clubs, social groups helping old people etc, and often served on committees, you would probably enjoy a job where you are meeting a lot of people and taking on a fair bit of responsibility.

(d) PERSONALITY

This is the deciding factor. Your shorthand and typing may be excellent, but if you are very shy and lacking in confidence there is no point going for a job in the front office of an advertising agency; you would be better off finding a small firm where your abilities are appreciated, but where you are not expected to meet and cope with new people all the time.

ASK YOURSELF:

- ☐ Are you a good mixer? What kind of people do you get on with?
- ☐ Do you get on easily with members of the opposite sex?
- ☐ Can you work as one of a team or do you prefer to get on with things on your own?
- ☐ Are you a natural organiser whom other people expect to get things done, or do you prefer to let someone else give the orders?
- ☐ Do you like a calm, organised life, with everything cut and dried, so that you know where you stand, or do you like a bit of drama and excitement?
- ☐ Do you panic when things go wrong, or are you the one who keeps cool and calm?
- ☐ Are you better with your hands than your brain?

Try to make an assessment of yourself as a person. How would you describe yourself to someone else? Scientific, creative, practical, open-air type, caring, literary, artistic — which of these adjectives applies to you?

Remember to allow for growing up, Lots of young people suffer from shyness and nervousness, but most of them learn to overcome (or at least conceal) this in time. So don't rule out a career that involves meeting a lot of people, perhaps even some public speaking, on that ground alone.

The main job types

Having thought about yourself a little, you must now go
through the list of job types and tick the points that you feel
apply to you. At the end, go back and see which type rates
the most ticks — that is, the one that fits most closely to
your personality. Some people, of course, will find that they
belong equally in two types — the practical and the executive
for example — and it is true that there is bound to be some
overlap. You will find more information about many of the
jobs suggested in Chapter 2. (Remember that specific jobs
may come under general headings, for example you will find
cookery under *catering* and *home economist*, and park keeper
under *local government*.)

THE PRACTICAL/TECHNICAL TYPE

- ☐ You would enjoy a skilled job that involved working
  with your hands or with tools and machinery.
- ☐ Your hobbies involve a lot of do-it-yourself, working
  with materials, working on practical projects, tinkering
  with machinery.
- ☐ You have craft or technical qualifications or CSEs or
  GCEs in practical subjects rather than academic ones.
- ☐ You are a calm, methodical person, not easily rattled.

POSSIBLE JOBS: Engineering apprenticeship; architectural
technician; building trades; dental technician; draughtsman;
laboratory technician; Merchant Navy (engineer or radio
officer); printing trade; animal technician; car mechanic;
meat industry; catering; British Rail engineer; Armed Forces
apprentice; woodwork; metalwork; plumbing; dressmaking;
cookery; painters and decorators; operating or maintenance
of office or factory machines; road transport and haulage.

THE EXECUTIVE TYPE

- ☐ Your qualifications are academic.
- ☐ You are 'good with people' and tend to be a natural

leader in almost any situation.

- ☐ You enjoy running things and taking decisions; you are an active member of various clubs and organisations.
- ☐ You have lots of confidence and initiative; you enjoy being with other people.
- ☐ You are a good speaker and committee-person; you are good at grasping facts and figures.

POSSIBLE JOBS: Banking; local government; legal executive; Civil Service; Health Service administration; public relations; personal assistant or secretary; insurance; accountancy; personnel management; store management; management training; estate agency; travel agent.

THE CREATIVE TYPE

- ☐ Your qualifications are probably in art, craft or language subjects.
- ☐ You are good with your hands and enjoy creative work with tools and materials.
- ☐ You are independent-minded, good at working on your own.
- ☐ You are highly imaginative.

POSSIBLE JOBS: Joining a craft workshop that specialises in hand-made jewellery, furniture etc; antique furniture repairing; picture restoring or framing; working in the design studio of an advertising agency, publisher or large company; fashion designer or pattern cutter; hairdressing; beautician; draughtsman; architectural technician; dressmaking; cookery; photography; journalism; illustrator; interior decoration; architecture.

THE OUTDOORS TYPE

- ☐ You enjoy either playing or watching sport.
- ☐ Your interests include swimming, walking, climbing, cycling etc.
- ☐ You are not very good at studying but learn best from watching others then having a go.
- ☐ You can keep calm and cheerful even when you are tired, cold or wet.

POSSIBLE JOBS: Forestry Commission; Merchant Navy; Armed

Forces; police; agriculture; gardening and horticulture; veterinary nurse; building trades; traffic warden; groundsman; park keeper, street cleaning and refuse collection; Outward Bound centres; zookeeper; physical education instructor; swimming instructor and lifesaver; road maintenance; car park attendant; motorbike messenger; postman; milkman.

THE CARING TYPE

- ☐ You enjoy being with other people.
- ☐ You help out in your spare time in youth clubs, old folk's homes etc.
- ☐ You like working with young children.
- ☐ You are patient and sympathetic.
- ☐ Other people's tantrums don't upset you.

POSSIBLE JOBS: Nursing; nursery nursing; social work; health therapy; hairdressing; teaching; home economics; speech therapy; physiotherapy; chiropody; audiology technician; Health Service administration; medical secretary; school secretary.

THE METHODICAL TYPE

- ☐ You are neat, tidy and well organised.
- ☐ You are good at attending to details.
- ☐ You have a strong sense of responsibility.
- ☐ You have a good head for figures.

POSSIBLE JOBS: Secretarial or clerical work; accounts clerk or accounts technician; library assistant; Civil Service; local government; legal technician; barrister's clerk (see Law); banking; travel and tourism; computer work; insurance; building society; office work; pharmacist; legal secretary.

THE SCIENTIFIC TYPE

- ☐ You have qualifications in mathematics and science subjects, in the academic rather than the technical field.
- ☐ Your hobbies and interests include chess, music, private research, finding out how things work, gadgetry of all kinds.

☐ You could be a team leader, but are not interested in being top dog at all times.

☐ You are naturally independent-minded, good at working on your own, calm and unexcitable.

POSSIBLE JOBS: Computer industry; accounting technician; laboratory technician; pharmacy technician; Civil Service (Science Group); animal technician; optician (dispensing); medical laboratory scientist; Armed Forces (engineering or electronic technician); home economist; engineering.

THE BOOKISH TYPE

☐ You have academic qualifications in the arts, languages, social studies.

☐ Your hobbies and interests are in the arts, reading, writing etc.

☐ You are not very interested in leading other people.

☐ You are much better at words than figures; you are good at expressing yourself either verbally or on paper.

POSSIBLE JOBS: Civil Service; local government; library assistant; legal executive; barrister's clerk; clerical work; Health Service administration; office work; publishing.

THE SALES TYPE

☐ You have little or no formal qualifications.

☐ You are 'good with people'.

☐ Other people admire your 'gift of the gab'.

☐ You have a quick mind and find it easy to think on your feet.

☐ You are very shrewd about money.

POSSIBLE JOBS: Sales assistant in a department store; trainee sales manager or trainee buyer in a store; public relations; demonstrator (see Home Economist); travel and tourism; sales representative; hotels and catering; estate agency.

There may be some people who feel that *none* of the job types apply to them. At this point, you probably need some professional advice to clear your mind and help you sort out what you would *like* to do, always remembering that the

chances of becoming a brain surgeon with only two O levels
are pretty slim.

Take some advice

Talk to as many people as you can while you are making up
your mind. Chat to your careers teacher at school and have a
look at the books available: they will give you some idea of
all the possibilities. Make sure you go to the careers activities
organised at school. Companies visit schools sometimes to
talk to pupils about the sort of work they do: they are
usually on the look-out for likely recruits and you should
make a point of going to such events just to see what the
options are.

There are also various professional advisers to whom you can
apply for further information or advice. These are: careers
teachers (guidance teachers in Scottish schools); careers
officers for people still at school or in further education and
also for those who have completed their education and want
to use the careers service; employment advisers at
employment offices and Jobcentres can also make
arrangements for interview by occupational guidance officers.
These services are for adults and young people who have left
school.

If you *still* don't know what to do, and are beginning to feel
desperate, it might be a good investment to consult one of
the professional advisory bodies — look in Yellow Pages
under 'Careers Advisory Services'. Not only do they give
exhaustive tests to find out what are your particular skills
and abilities (the results may surprise you — many people
have quite erroneous beliefs about their own abilities) but
they also find out about your interests and preferences. All
your qualifications and ability tests may point towards a job
in accountancy, but if balance sheets bore you to tears there
is not much point taking a job just to please the family. The
professional adviser may be able to suggest some other use for
your abilities which is more in line with your general interests.

References

More often than not you are asked to give references

whatever the type of job for which you are applying, so it is well to have them organised in advance. References are assurances of your character — basically that you are honest, reliable, and hardworking.

FOR SCHOOL-LEAVERS

They should be responsible people respected in the community with whom you have had some contact and who are therefore able to judge you: professional people such as teachers (preferably the head teacher), the local priest/ clergyman/head of religious group, scoutmaster or bank manager. Or you could ask someone you have done a holiday job for, such as a local shopkeeper. Referees should *not* be related to you and it is not a good idea to ask somebody simply because he/she is a friend. Always check beforehand that someone is prepared to give a reference. Tell them as much as you can about the job — that will help them to write something suitable.

FOR PEOPLE CHANGING JOBS

If you have already had a job, at least one referee will have to be someone who can vouch for your work record: either the head of the firm, or your works supervisor or the head of department where you worked.

Changing your job

Perhaps you are already in a job and have just decided that you made a terrible mistake. Your boss is a tyrant; the work is drudgery; getting up to go to work in the morning has become a nightmare.

Even if it is as bad as that, don't just give in at the end of the first week, even if you are free to do so. *Any* first job, however awful, should be given two weeks, and ideally a month. You must allow for the fact that it is all new and strange — knuckling down to the authority of anyone, however nice, can be a strain. Most people feel exhausted after their first day in a new job, however many jobs they have had. So give yourself time to settle in, and if you still feel the same at the end of the fortnight — take advice.

DON'T just rush to hand in your notice. Talk it over with someone whose judgement you trust — your parents, the careers officer at school, other people at work.

If, after all that, you still feel the same and do hand in your notice — don't feel guilty. It's easy to make a mistake when you have no experience of jobs. No one is pretending that all jobs are lovely — some *are* badly paid drudgery and no one is going to blame you for getting out, quite the reverse. So when you go to your next interview and are asked why you stayed such a short time, tell the truth. You made a terrible mistake, realised it in time, and got out quickly. Next time you are going to look a bit more closely at the job and what it has to offer before you rush to accept.

Chapter 2

JOB GUIDE

In this chapter we give an alphabetical list of the main job areas, including such major employers as the Civil Service, the Armed Forces and local government. The list is not meant to be exhaustive — there are hundreds of different jobs — but we have covered all the main areas of work open to young people.

In each case we have given a brief job description, together with entry qualifications required, if any, and any training you can do. We also tell you where to write for further information and where to look for jobs.

ACCOUNTANCY

Accounts Clerk, Bookkeeper, Accounting Technician, Accountant

In these jobs you work in the accounts departments of industrial or commercial companies, or perhaps in local government which employs a lot of clerical staff. You will be expected to have at least O level maths, and it is an advantage to have taken elementary bookkeeping or commercial subjects at school.

Accounting technicians work at an intermediate level in the accounts departments of industry, commerce, the public sector and private accountancy practices, often in a managerial capacity.

Membership of the Association of Accounting Technicians (AAT) is the recognised qualification. The minimum requirements for registration as an AAT student are four GCE O levels, Scottish Ordinary grades, or grade 1 CSEs, in maths or statistics, English language, and not more than one craft subject. Success in the AAT's examinations or approved equivalents, together with three years' proven experience of accounting work, will make you eligible for membership of the AAT.

Work in accounts departments increasingly involves the use of computers and information processors, and the examinations of the AAT cover data processing and systems analysis for use with computerised systems as well as such traditional subjects as law and taxation.

Further information

Association of Accounting Technicians (AAT)
21 Jockeys Field
London WC1R 4BN
01-405 4961

Association of Cost and Executive Accountants
141 Fonthill Road
London N4 3HF
01-272 3925

The Chartered Association of Certified Accountants
29 Lincoln's Inn Fields
London WC2A 3EE
01-242 6855

Institute of Chartered Accountants in England and Wales (ACA)
Chartered Accountants' Hall
Moorgate Place
London EC2P 2BJ
01-628 7060

Institute of Chartered Accountants of Scotland (CA)
27 Queen Street
Edinburgh EH2 1LA
031-225 5673

Institute of Cost and Management Accountants (ACMA)
63 Portland Place
London W1N 4AB
01-637 2311

Careers in Accountancy, Kogan Page

Where to look for jobs

The Accountant (weekly)
Certified Accountant (monthly)
Daily Telegraph
Management Accounting (monthly)
Municipal Journal (weekly)
Local papers, particularly evening papers
Opportunities (weekly) for public service jobs
Accounting Technician (monthly)

AGRICULTURE

There is an enormous range of jobs in this field and, for most of them, no entry qualifications are needed. You can get a job working with livestock (cattle, dairy cows, pigs, poultry or sheep) straight from school.

The first thing you will be asked to do is learn how to drive a tractor — large farms will have at least one farm mechanic, but otherwise you will have to be able to cope with running repairs to machinery. Hours are generally long and irregular and you have to like working on your own. If you want a more responsible or better-paid job, you can take a National Certificate. Exams for these are taken at the end of the one-year full-time courses run by agricultural and horticultural colleges and are intended for students (aged 16 and over) who want to become farm foremen, head stockmen or farmers in their own right. Most courses require you to have spent at least one year working on a farm to gain practical experience. Entry requirement is a good education to GCE or CSE standard, including English, maths and science. There are also training programmes organised by the Agricultural Training Board for people who are already in full-time work. Applicants can be beginners, YTS trainees, or more experienced people who want to learn new skills. Training can be organised through a formal apprenticeship, leading to the Agricultural Training Board Certificate. *See also* Gardening and Horticulture, and the Forestry Commission.

Further information

Agricultural Training Board
Bourne House
32-34 Beckenham Road
Beckenham
Kent BR3 4PB
01-650 4890

National Farmers' Union
Agriculture House
Knightsbridge
London SW1X 7NJ
01-235 5077

Royal Association of British Dairy Farmers
Robarts House
Rossmore Road
London NW1 6NP
01-723 7304

Careers Education and Training Advice Centre
The National Agricultural Centre
Stoneleigh
Kenilworth
Warwickshire CV8 2LZ
0203 555100

Careers in Agriculture and Agricultural Sciences, Kogan Page

Where to look for jobs

Farmer's Weekly (weekly) for all farming jobs
British Farmer and Stockbreeder (fortnightly) for stockmen, tractor drivers, pigmen, herdsmen etc

ANIMAL TECHNICIAN

The animal technician looks after animals used in research in medicine, veterinary science and the pharmaceutical industry, helps to carry out experiments and reports on results. The technician must be fond of animals and good at handling them, but must also not be squeamish.

Training is done on the job. There are no specific entry requirements, though a good standard of biology or zoology is preferable and most laboratories will expect at least two O levels in science subjects. Trainees study on the job part-time for the examinations of the Institute of Animal Technicians.

Further information

Institute of Animal Technicians
5 South Parade
Oxford OX2 7JL

Careers Working with Animals, Kogan Page

ARCHITECTURAL TECHNICIAN

The architectural technician works in an architect's office, either in a private practice or for a local authority. The job involves collecting and preparing technical information; preparing technical drawings for builders and clients; liaising with clients and with surveyors and attending meetings on site with builders.

Entry qualifications are four O levels, including maths, a science subject and a subject showing a grasp of written English. You obviously need to be able to draw and have an eye for detail. Training is given on the job with day-release to qualify for the ONC in Building, followed by the BTEC equivalent.

Further information

Society of Architectural and Associated Technicians
397 City Road
London EC1V 1NE
01-278 2206

Careers in Architecture, Kogan Page

Where to look for jobs

Local press

THE ARMED FORCES

THE ARMY

The Army is one of the major employers in this country. It can train
you to work in a wide variety of occupations, making use of whatever
natural talents you possess. If you have technical ability, you can
become an apprentice in one of the many trades available; if you are
musical, you will be given a training in that too. Entry qualifications
include a medical examination, an aptitude test, and a fitness test at the
Selection Centre.

Junior Entry

You can join the Junior Army as soon as you are legally old enough to
leave school. There are four categories of junior entry:

Junior Leaders (entry age 15 years 11 months - 17)
The training in Junior Leader Regiments is designed to develop the
qualities needed in future Warrant Officers and NCOs of the Army,
particularly those who belong to front line units. The training, which
lasts for 12 months, concentrates on the development of character and
leadership. It is also designed to provide further general education and
specialised military skills.

Junior Soldiers (entry age 16 years 6 months - 17)
The training is similar to that for Junior Leaders, but there is less
emphasis on leadership. Junior Soldiers who develop leadership
qualities after they enlist are given opportunities for promotion after
basic training; some are transferred to Junior Leader training when their
performance merits it.

As a Junior Soldier, a young man will have a head start in the Army: by
the time he is 17½ he will be a fully trained soldier able to take his place

in the Arm or Corps of his choice. However, he cannot be sent on active service till he is 18.

Junior Bandsmen (entry age 15 years 11 months - 17½)
The Army trains its own musicians at the Army Schools of Music, and the best way to start is as a Junior Bandsman. Previous experience is preferable but not essential and you must be auditioned by a Director of Music. Initial training, at one of the Junior Schools of Music, at Bovington or Pirbright, takes up to two years and includes further general education. Those who show special aptitude may be given a 12-month course at the Royal Military School of Music, Kneller Hall, Twickenham.

Army Apprentices (entry age 15 years 8 months - 17½)
Army Apprentices' Colleges are at Arborfield, Chepstow, Harrogate and Aldershot. They provide a very high standard of technical training for the young man who has shown some ability in scientific, mathematical and manual subjects at school. The training varies slightly at each college and, in the early stages, is designed to test the aptitude of an apprentice for the trade of his choice. The choice is wide, from electronics to bricklaying and training lasts two years.

The college that an apprentice will attend depends on the result of his selection interview, his own preferences, and the type of training that he will need. No special academic qualifications are needed, but boys should be encouraged to sit relevant CSE or O levels. Graduates of the apprentices' colleges provide the Army with most of its highly skilled and well-paid technicians.

Terms of service

Young men who join the Junior Army enlist on a Notice Engagement. You agree to serve from the time your training starts until your 18th birthday and thereafter for six or nine years depending on training. If you are not suited to Army life you can leave at no cost within the first six months of joining. At the age of 18, you are given the opportunity to confirm your six- or nine-year engagement or to reduce it, but the minimum period allowable from the age of 18 is three years. Because of the length of training, which may take you past your 18th birthday, all Apprentices and Junior Bandsmen are required to serve for at least three years from the end of training.

The Guaranteed Vacancy Scheme

Once you have successfully completed the entire selection process, the Army will guarantee you a place at a suitable junior training unit and will award you a Guaranteed Vacancy Certificate. The vacancy is finally confirmed once parental consent has been given, but you must maintain your medical and character standards.

The scheme is particularly important if you apply during your final year at school as you are then assured of an Army career before you leave school. However, the scheme remains open for those who have left, providing they will not be over the maximum age limits at the time of their subsequent enlistment.

The Army will keep a vacancy open but you can change your mind at any time up to the moment you enlist.

The Selection Centre

At the Selection Centre you will be given a detailed briefing on the jobs and training which the Army has to offer, together with written aptitude tests to discover what type of job would best suit you. You will also be interviewed by an Army Personnel Selection Officer. The Army will pay all your travel expenses and will accommodate and feed you during your visit.

Adult entry (male) (entry age 17 - 25)

GENERAL

Before being enlisted or committed to joining the Army in any way, applicants must attend a two-day selection briefing at the Army Personnel Selection Centre, Sutton Coldfield, or at Edinburgh. During their stay which is free, they take a written ability test and are then briefed on all army jobs that they are eligible for. It is then up to the applicant, with the assistance of a Personnel Selection Officer, to choose which type of employment he wants. If he does not like any of the jobs offered to him, he can cancel his application. If he does choose one, he returns home to be enlisted subsequently at his Army Recruiting Office. He then proceeds to his training unit. All training starts with nine weeks' common military training and continues with more specialist work either at another training establishment or in the unit concerned.

Technicians
As the Army goes into new fields of technical development there are more and more opportunities for technically minded young men in important and interesting jobs. Young men training in key trades such as avionics, aircraft, radar, guided weapons, control equipment, instruments, telecommunications, survey, aircraft, construction, mechanical and electrical engineering are now forming the nucleus of an increasingly progressive modern Army. The pay is good right from the start and training is in some of the best-equipped workshops in the country. Training is both practical and theoretical and lasts up to two years.

Artificer entry scheme
Men up to the age of 30 who have served an apprenticeship in a

27

mechanical electrical or electronics trade and have reached ONC or an equivalent standard may apply to enlist to fill supervisory appointments as Artificers. Those accepted by the interview board start as Sergeants and are given 18 months' further training. On successful completion of this they are promoted to Staff Sergeant.

Adult entry (female) (entry age 17¼ - 33)

Women's Royal Army Corps (WRAC)
The WRAC offers girls a choice of more than 20 jobs to learn, final course allocation depending on aptitude and individual choice. All start by being given six weeks' basic training and then they move on to learn their chosen job with one of the Army Regiments or Corps. Opportunities exist for radar operators, police work, drivers, typists, cooks, telephonists, etc. A good all-round educational standard is required, and in some jobs GCE O level is needed.

You are encouraged to continue your education and may be given time off for study. There is no compulsion to do so, but promotion normally depends on passing examinations.

Queen Alexandra's Royal Army Nursing Corps (QARANC)
Girls who have a minimum of five GCE O levels (or equivalent), which must include English language and a science subject plus two other academic subjects (mathematics is recommended), may be trained in the QARANC to become Registered General Nurses.

Girls who have two O levels, which must include English language and one other academic subject, may be trained to become Enrolled Nurses (General). Opportunities also exist for qualified Enrolled Nurses (General) as vacancies occur, and qualified physiotherapists. Girls who do not wish to nurse but are interested in hospital work may choose to be trained as medical clerks, dental clerk assistants, ward stewardesses, pharmacy technicians or radiographers.

Further information

Contact your local Army Careers Information Office (in the phone one book under 'Army').

Careers in the Army, Kogan Page

ROYAL NAVY

The Royal Navy is the second largest navy in NATO, and plays a major role in the support of the Western Alliance and in national defence. It has a modern fleet of surface warships, fixed-wing aircraft and helicopters, supported by a large number of repair, maintenance and replenishment vessels. The Navy is equally formidable underwater: the Submarine Service has nuclear-powered and conventional submarines and with Polaris submarines on patrol the Navy is responsible for Britain's contribution to the strategic deterrent of the Western Alliance.

There is a great variety, both in the kind of job available and in the type of vessel on which you could serve. You might be on an aircraft carrier, assault ship, guided missile destroyer, frigate, minesweeper, patrol vessel, survey ship, tanker or fishery protection vessel. There is the possibility of serving in the Fleet Air Arm or in the Submarine Service. And a wide choice of specialist training is open to you, from radar and electronic warfare through to supply and secretariat functions.

Operations branch

In order to join you must be between 16 and 33, and able to pass a medical examination and a selection test. Those under 17½ join as a Junior; otherwise as Ordinary Rating. All ratings do their basic training at HMS Raleigh.

The expertise and skills provided by the Operations Branch cover such a wide range of duties that the branch splits into two groups — the Seaman and the Communications Group. The former provides the skills and techniques required to 'work' and 'fight' a ship which among other things includes an expert knowledge of seamanship and of ship's weaponry. The Communications Group, as the name implies, is expert in a wide range of communcations systems from radio teletype equipment to morse telegraphy or signalling lights for ship-to-ship communication.

On completion of basic training, men of the Seaman Group sub-specialise in one of the following for which they are further trained:

SEAMAN GROUP

Electronic Warfare (EW) — Concerned with the electronic equipment in Operations Rooms used to intercept 'enemy' transmissions.

Radar (R) — Working in the Operations Rooms of ships on warning radar, ie plotting positions of ships and aircraft.

Missile (M) — The control and operation of ships' weapons.

Sonar (Surface ships) and Sonar (Submarines) — Operating sonar equipment to hunt submarines and surface ships.

Diver (D) — Working in teams during fleet exercises; mine disposal and mine clearance, experimental diving.

Mine Warfare (MW) — Service in mine countermeasures vessels.

Survey Recorder (SR) — Compiling of information needed for Admiralty Charts.

Tactical Systems (Submarines) — Navigation, enemy detection by radar, computer-assisted plotting.

Those attached to the *Communications Group* of the Operations Branch sub-specialise (after basic training) in one of the following duties for which they are further trained:

COMMUNICATIONS GROUP

Radio Operator (Tactical) — Expert in message handling systems and in communications procedures, relating to the tactical movement of ships.

Radio Operator (Submarine) — Expert in all types of communication systems used in conventional and nuclear submarines.

Radio Operator (General) — Concerned with all types of radio equipment both long and short range with the handling of general signal traffic and the provision of radio equipment for other tactical user departments in the ship.

Engineering Branch

Artificers — These are the most skilled engineering technicians in the Royal Navy. If equipment breaks down in a ship or an aircraft, or if machinery is damaged, it is the judgement and skill of the Artificer which counts in getting it working properly again in the shortest possible time. There are three categories in which Artificers serve: *Air Engineering Artificer, Marine Engineering Artificer, Weapon Engineering Artificer.*

Entry
Artificer apprentices receive a five-year training. They must pass a selection test, aptitude tests, interview, medical examination and qualify in a special written examination. (Exemption from the examination may be gained by obtaining GCE O level at Grade C or above in physics, maths and English language, or by completing the first year of a BTEC Certificate or Diploma in Engineering, or by equivalent qualifications.) Age limits: 16 - 21.

Those who have taken an appropriate engineering apprenticeship may be eligible to apply for direct entry. Age limits: 19½ - 33.

Mechanics — Within the engineering branch it is also possible to become a *Marine Engineering Mechanic, Weapon Engineering Mechanic*, or *Air Engineering Mechanic*. Entry qualifications: selection test, interview and medical examination.

Medical Branch

Medical Technician — Must have GCE O level passes, or equivalent, in at least five subjects. For some Medical Technician specialisations one or two A levels are required.

You are given three years' training in Naval Hospitals, and must pass examinations and obtain civilian qualifications in one of the following:

Radiography, Laboratory (General), Environmental Health Inspector, Pharmacy Dispenser. Direct entry as a Physiotherapist or as a Medical Technician in any of the above specialisms is also open to men who already hold the appropriate qualifications.

Medical Assistant — 13 weeks' initial training is followed by 32 weeks' practical training on the wards and in medical departments. Successful completion leads to the City and Guilds Certificate in Basic Medical Services. Further specialisation possible as Submarine Medical Assistant, Commando Medical Assistant, Dental Surgery Assistant, Operating Department Assistant or in other medical specialisations. Entry qualifications: selection test, interview and medical examination.

Supply and Secretarial Branch

CATERING

In the Royal Navy catering embraces a wide range of skills which include cooking, baking, marketing, valeting, table service, accounting and stock control.

The combined expertise of three types of specialists — Cooks, Stewards and Catering Accountants — provide these skills at sea and ashore all over the world, also in the UK and home waters. Entry into any one of these three specialisms ensures a professional training which can lead to qualifications recognised by the City and Guilds Institute.

Cook — Naval cooks are trained to high standards in a wide range of culinary skills. The provision of good food to a ship's company is vital to their well being and the efficiency of the ship and the role of the cook is consequently most important.

Steward — Naval stewards serve, and sometimes prepare food and drink in the wardroom (the officers' mess) in ships and shore establishments.

Catering Accountant — Catering accountants are responsible for deciding on exactly what provisions will be needed and working out the cost of food.

CLERICAL WORK

Stores Accountant — 50,000 separate items could be needed by a ship and her crew at sea. The Stores Accountant has to ensure that the right stores are carried, kept in good condition and are available at a moment's notice.

Writer — Involves clerical duties in the pay, cash and administrative offices of ships, submarines and shore establishments.

Entry qualifications for all the above: selection test, interview and medical examination.

FLEET AIR ARM

Naval Airman — Helps to control and direct the movements of aircraft, and to ensure their safety at all times. Specialisations in aircraft handling, survival equipment, meteorology.

Entry qualifications: selection test, interview and medical examination. For Naval Airman (Meteorology) you must be over 17½ and have one GCE O level (or equivalent) in maths, meteorology, geography or a science subject.

OFFICER CAREERS

There is also a very wide choice of roles for naval officers — as Seaman Officer, Engineer Officer, Supply and Secretariat Officer, Instructor, and the various sub-specialisms. Minimum qualifications are five GCE O levels (or equivalent), including maths, English language, and a physics-based science. Many officers join after taking a degree. Age limits in most cases are 17 - 26.

ROYAL MARINES

The Royal Marines have a long history of daring action as part of the Royal Navy, fighting the enemy from Royal Navy ships and taking part in almost every major sea battle until the end of the last century. In recent times they have gained a new role as Commandos, working from ships and aircraft to fight on land, and they receive specialist training in jungle, mountain and arctic warfare.

If you are interested in joining the Royal Marines, attending a two-day *Potential Recruits Course* will give you a taste of what the life is like. You can then join at one of the following levels:

Junior Marine — General Duties with Royal Marines Commando Units and Ships of the Fleet, following specialised training at Commando Training Centre, Lympstone. No operational service ashore or afloat before age 18.

You must pass a 'pull up' test, medical examination, selection test (reasoning, arithmetic, English language and mechanical comprehension) and Potential Recruits Course.

Marine — (Age 17½ - 28 on entry) Royal Marines General Duties and Technical Branches. Following specialised Commando Training at Commando Training Centre, Lympstone, you serve in Commando Units and Ships of the Fleet.

You must pass a 'pull-up' test medical examination, selection test (reasoning, arithmetic, English language and mechanical comprehension) and Potential Recruits Course.

For those who have completed their Commando Training there are many specialist options such as the *Air Squadron* or the *Special Boat*

Squadron, and the chance to train in trades such as Driver, Vehicle Mechanic, Metalsmith, Illustrator, Carpenter and Joiner.

It is also possible to join the Royal Marine Band Service. To enter as a *Junior Musician* or *Junior Bugler* you must be 16-17½, and pass the usual tests plus a test of musical aptitude. Fully trained musicians (aged 17½-28) are also accepted.

WOMEN'S ROYAL NAVAL SERVICE (WRNS)

Members of the Women's Royal Naval Service serve in naval bases, Command and NATO Headquarters, Royal Marines training establishments, Naval Air Stations, at the Ministry of Defence in Whitehall at NATO Headquarters in Belgium, Italy, Norway and Portugal, and with naval detachments in Gibralter and Hong Kong. Although they do not serve at sea, they play an important part in helping to keep the Navy's shore organisation and the fleet operating efficiently.

RATING ENTRY (Entry age 17-28)

Ratings do five weeks' basic training followed by specialist training in the appropriate training establishment. They work in the United Kingdom and in some establishments abroad, and serve on a Notice Engagement with opportunity for re-engagement. Candidates undergo an aptitude test and must pass a medical examination. In certain categories, GCE O level or equivalent standard of education is required. There are different job opportunities according to qualifications, aptitude and service requirements at the time of entry. WRNS ratings help to staff communications centres and do much of the Navy's clerical and accounting work. They maintain and repair naval aircraft, drive a wide variety of service vehicles, plot naval air and sea exercises, and assist in the preparation of meteorological information. They cook, issue stores, are stewards, photographers, educational assistants, operate audio-visual equipment, assist dental surgeons and operate switchboards.

CADET ENTRY

This method of joining is for girls who want to be considered for officer training. You need 5 GCE O level passes (or equivalent) including English and maths, with two passes at A level, normally Grade C or above (or 3 SCE Higher Grade passes).

Basic and specialist training is followed by 12-15 months as a rating. Near the end of this time you attend the Selection Board for Officer candidates. If successful, you go forward for officer training.

DIRECT ENTRY (Entry age 20½-26½)

This is for graduates and those with certain professional qualifications, entering as officers.

QUEEN ALEXANDRA'S ROYAL NAVAL NURSING SERVICE (QARNNS)

Queen Alexandra's Royal Naval Nursing Service is an important part of the Royal Naval Medical Service which is primarily responsible for the health of men and women in the Royal Navy, the Royal Marines and the Women's Royal Naval Service. It also cares for dockyard employees, the families of officers and men accommodated overseas and civilians who are admitted to naval hospitals in the United Kingdom by arrangement with the National Health Service. Over 26 establishments at home and abroad have complements of QARNNS nurses. These may vary from the big base hospital to air stations of the Fleet Air Arm with small sick bays.

The scope of the work is similar to that in any civilian district general hospital or medical centre, and offers the qualified nurse a wide range of experience and variety.

Entry
Minimum age 18. For RGN training you need at least five O levels or their equivalent in academic subjects. For EN training you do not need O levels but you may be asked to pass the Naval Educational Test. All naval nurses are required to pass a medical examination and selection test.

Youth Training Scheme
Like the other services, the Navy is taking part in the Youth Training Scheme. Further details are available from the RN and RM Careers Information Offices listed below.

Further information

Information about career opportunities in the Royal Navy, Royal Marines, QARNNS or WRNS may be obtained by writing to one of the offices listed below.

Aberdeen: 63 Belmont Street, AB1 1JS
Belfast: 16 Howard Street, BT1 6PA
Birmingham: Unit 46, Birmingham Shopping Centre, B2 4XD
Blackburn: 46 Church Street, BB1 5AL
Blackheath: 9 Lee Road, SE3 9RQ
Brighton: 34 Queen's Road, BN1 3XB
Bristol: Esso Building, 35 Colston Avenue, BS1 4TY
Cambridge: 90-92 Regent Street, CB2 1DP
Canterbury: 17 St Peter's Street, CT1 2BG
Cardiff: 11 St David's House, Wood Street, CF1 1PE
Carlisle: 19 Warwick Road, CA1 1DH
Chatham: 1 Dock Road, ME4 4JR
Chelmsford: 2 Park Way, CM2 0SG
Coventry: First Floor, Broadgate House, Upper Precinct, CV1 1NU
Croydon: 18 Park Street, CR10 1YE
Derby: 96 Green Lane, DE1 1RR *or* 31 Castlefields Main Centre, DE1 2PE

Doncaster: 80 Cleveland Street, DN1 3DP
Dorchester: Georgian House, Trinity Street, DT1 1UD
Dundee: 49 Overgate, DD1 1QQ
Edinburgh: 49 Lothian Road, EH1 2DN
Exeter: Fountain House, Western Way, EX1 2DQ
Glasgow: 94 West Nile Street, G1 2QW *or* Charlotte House, 78 Queen
    Street, G1 3DN
Guildford: 20 Chertsey Street, GU1 4HF
Hartlepool: 223 York Road, TS26 9AD
Hull: Town Centre House, 85 Prospect Street, HU2 8PF
Ilford: 180A Cranbrook Road, Greater London IG1 4LB
Invernes: 3 Bridge Street, IV1 1HG
Ipswich: 58 Princes Street, IP1 1RJ
Leeds: 36 Wellington Street, LS1 2DL
Leicester: 84–86 Charles Street, LE1 1FB
Lincoln: 17 Saltergate, LN2 1DH
Liverpool: Graeme House, Derby Square, Red Cross Street, L2 7SD
London: State House, High Holborn, WC1R 4TG
Luton: 18–19 West Side Centre, off Dunstable Road, LU1 1EF
Manchester: Townbury House, Blackfriars Street, Salford M3 5AF
Milton Keynes: 8 Wetherburn Court, Brunel Centre, MK2 2UH
Newcastle upon Tyne: Gunner House, Neville Street, NE1 5HD
Northampton: Newilton House, Derngate, NN1 1TY
Norwich: 45 Prince of Wales Road, NR1 1BL
Nottingham: 70 Milton Street, Victoria Centre, NG1 3QX
Oxford: 35 St Giles, OX1 3LJ
Peterborough: 23 Hereward Centre, PE1 1TB
Plymouth: 117 Mayflower Street, PL1 1SD
Portsmouth: 41 Arundel Street, PO1 1ND
Preston: 83A Fishergate, PR1 2NJ
Reading: 13 Kings Road, RG1 3AR
Sheffield: Castle Market, S1 1FZ
Shrewsbury: 7–8 St Mary's Street, SY1 1EB
Southampton: 151 High Street, SO9 4PB
St Helens: 7 George Street, WA10 1DA
Stoke on Trent: 3 Charles Street, Hanley, ST1 3JP
Sunderland: 4 Burdon Road, SR1 1QB
Swansea: 17–19 Castle Street, SA1 1JF
Swindon: 18 Milton Road, SN1 5JN
Truro: 107 Kenwyn Street, TR1 3DJ
Watford: 35 St Alban's Road, WD1 1SH
Wolverhampton: 23 Victoria Street, WV1 3PB
Worcester: 42 Broad Street, WR1 3LR
Wrexham: 21 Rhosddu Road, LL11 1NF
York: 4 New Street, YO1 2RA

RAF/WRAF

The RAF doesn't just consist of men who fly. Getting an aircraft into the air, keeping it up there and bringing it down again safely depends on a lot of skilled men and women down on the ground. An RAF station is rather like a small town where everyone works for the same firm. There are skilled people to service and maintain the aircraft, to look after their instrumentation, to plot their course. In turn these people depend on other skilled people to feed them, clothe them, look after their health, instruct them and protect them, all of which means many different jobs, trades and skills to keep the RAF fully operational. For a full list of all the RAF/WRAF trades, see the table on page 38.

For most trades you need no formal qualifications. All they ask is that you are between 16½ (17 for girls) and 39 — which means a chance to start a new career if you have already been working for a few years. However, they will expect you to be medically fit, although you can still wear glasses in the majority of trades.

Girls have the choice of many trades and have the same opportunities for advancement as the men. Also, in almost every trade, airmen and airwomen work closely together during and after trade training. If you haven't yet decided on a trade, the RAF Careers Information Office will find out the things you like to do and take into account any qualifications you may have. Then they will ask you to take their special aptitude tests.

While the majority of trades require no entry qualifications, the RAF does welcome people with O levels and for certain specialised technical trades GCEs or equivalent in mathematics and physics are essential. If you have four O levels including mathematics and a science subject, and are between 16 and 18½ (exceptionally 21), you could apply for an apprenticeship.

Engineering

There are three levels of engineering skills within the RAF — Mechanic, Technician and Engineering Technician. It is possible to work in most engineering trade groups at any one of these three levels. All three are involved with the same equipment or aspects of an aircraft. The main difference between them is the training you receive and the work you are expected to do. Once you have decided on the trade you would like to specialise in you can work out which level to apply for.

MECHANIC

If you do not have the qualifications for entry as a Technician, the way to start would be as a Mechanic. You may think that mechanics only work on cars. Some do, certainly, but in the RAF it is a traditional title that applies to all engineering trades. For example, it is possible to be a Mechanic specialising in electronics, aircraft engines or communications.

Basically, a Mechanic is someone who has been given a thorough training in his trade and will usually work alongside a more experienced Technician. You would be doing a useful job and gaining experience as you go along. Later you may qualify to be selected for training as a Technician.

TECHNICIAN

To join the RAF as a Technician you need GCE O levels in maths and physics at Grade C or above, or equivalent qualifications. Alternatives such as BTEC or City and Guilds will be considered.

Depending on your trade, your training course will last between nine and 18 months, and at the end you will be equipped to work as one of a team of RAF specialists.

ENGINEERING TECHNICIAN

The way to become an Engineering Technician is through an RAF Apprenticeship (see below).

Apprenticeships

You can take an RAF Apprenticeship in aircraft engineering or electronics. Both are three-year courses. Age limits are 16 - 18½ (exceptionally up to 21).

AIRCRAFT ENGINEERING TECHNICIAN (AIRFRAMES/PROPULSION)

This trade involves you in the maintenance, repair and servicing of a very wide range of airframes, engines and mechanical and hydraulic systems. You go to the School of Technical Training at RAF Halton, near Wendover, Bucks, on a course lasting about three years.

When you qualify you will be capable of working on all types of aircraft, making regular checks on the aircraft structure, inspecting the gas-turbine engines and propulsion systems. You will have knowledge of all types of flying controls, power-operated controls, landing gear, flaps and dive brakes, and you will also know what is right or wrong with the hydraulic systems used for their operation. You will also work on the many mechanical systems such as fuel, oil, de-icing, air-conditioning and cabin pressurisation. Then there is oxygen, engine and propeller control plus helicopter rotors and transmission.

When you finish you will be a Junior Technician with a BTEC qualification.

If you are more interested in the electronics side of things, you have a choice of apprenticeships. You can apply to become an Electronic Engineering Technician specialising in flight systems, or an Electronic Engineering Technician specialising in air communications and air radar.

	No of O levels or CSE equivalents required	Minimum age RAF	Minimum age WRAF
Aircraft Engineering Technician (Propulsion/Airframe)	4*	16	—
Aircraft Technician (Airframe)	2*	16½	17
Aircraft Mechanic (Airframe)	—	16½	17
Aircraft Technician (Propulsion)	2*	16½	17
Aircraft Mechanic (Propulsion)	—	16½	17
Aircraft Technician (Weapons)	2*	16½	17
Aircraft Mechanic (Weapons)	—	16½	17
Aircraft Technician (Electrical)	2*	16½	17
Aircraft Mechanic (Electrical)	—	16½	17
Electronics Engineering Technician (Air Communications/Air Radar)	4*	16	—
Electronics Technician (Air Communications)	2*	16½	17
Electronics Mechanic	—	16½	17
Electronics Technician (Air Radar)	2*	16½	17
Electronics Mechanic (Air Radar)	—	16½	17
Electronics Technician (Air Defence)	2*	16½	17
Electronics Mechanic (Air Defence)	—	16½	17
Electronics Engineering Technician (Flight Systems)	4*	16	17
Electronics Technician (Flight Systems)	2*	16½	17
Electronics Mechanic (Flight Systems)	—	16½	17
Electronics Technician (Airfield)	2*	16½	17
Electronics Mechanic (Airfield)	—	16½	—
Electronics Technician (Synthetic Trainer)	2*	16½	17
Electronics Technician (Telecommunications)	2*	16½	17
Electronics Mechanic (Telecommunications)	—	16½	17
General Technician (Ground Support Equipment)	2*	16½	17
General Mechanic (Ground Support Equipment)	—	16½	17
General Technician (Workshops)	2*	16½	17
General Mechanic (Workshops)	—	16½	17
General Technician (Electrical)	2*	16½	17
General Mechanic (Electrical)	—	16½	17
Carpenter	—	16½	17
Aerial Erector	—	16½	—
Mechanical Transport Driver	—	17	17
Mechanical Transport Technician	2*	16½	17
Mechanical Transport Mechanic	—	16½	17
RAF Police	—	17½	18½
Kennelmaid	—	—	17

*Engineering trades require maths and an acceptable science subject with a physics base. SCE arithmetic is *not* acceptable in lieu of GCE O level maths.
†For professionally-qualified entrants, the GCE requirement is waived.

Summary of jobs available and entry requirements

	No of O levels or CSE equivalents required	Minimum age RAF	Minimum age WRAF
RAF Regiment Gunner	—	17	—
Fireman	—	17½	—
Assistant Air Traffic Controller	—	16½	17
Physical Training Instructor	—	17½	18½
WRAF Administrative	—	18	18
RAF General Duties	—	16½	17
Telecommunications Operator	—	16½	17
Telephonist	—	16½	17
Radio Operator (Voice)	—	18	18
Special Telegraphist	—	18	18
Aerospace Systems Operator	—	16½	17
Survival Equipment Fitter	—	16½	17
Painter and Finisher	—	16½	17
Air Cartographer	—	16½	17
Plotter Air Photography	—	16½	17
Air Photography Processor 2	—	16½	17
Photographer (Ground)	—	18	18
Administrative Clerk	—	16½	17
Data Analyst	—	16½	17
WRAF Shorthand Typist (Qualified)	—	—	17
WRAF Typist (Qualified)	—	—	17
Musician	—	16½	—
Enrolled Nurse (General)	—	20	20
Pupil Nurse (General)	2	17¾	17¾
Laboratory Technician	5†	16½	17
Physiotherapist (Qualified)		21	21
Mental Nurse	4†	18	18
Medical Assistant		16½	17
Environmental Health Technician	3†	17½	17½
Operating Theatre Technician	2†	16½	17
Electrophysiological Technician	5†	16½	17
Pharmacy Technician	5†	16½	17
Radiographer	3 + 1 A†	18	18
Dental Hygienist	2†	17	17
Dental Surgery Assistant		16½	17
Dental Technician	4†	16½	17
Supplier	—	16½	17
Movements Operator	—	16½	—
Cook	—	16½	17
Catering Clerk	—	16½	17
Steward/Stewardess	—	16½	17

Both these apprenticeships are carried out at the School of Technical Training at RAF Cosford, near Wolverhampton, and the courses last three years.

ELECTRONIC ENGINEERING (FLIGHT SYSTEMS)

For this trade you will work on all the equipment associated with flight stability and control plus navigation and weapon aiming. This includes auto-stabilising systems, flight directors, military flight systems, auto pilots, inertial navigation systems, combined nav/attack systems and radio navigation aids. This equipment also comprises gyros, servo-mechanisms, analogue and digital computers and various counters.

ELECTRONIC ENGINEERING TECHNICIAN (AIR COMMUNICATIONS/ AIR RADAR)

If you choose this trade you will learn to maintain all the air communications and air radar equipment used in the RAF. This involves weather radar, distance measuring instruments; radio altimeters, long- and short-range communications equipment, radio compasses, hyperbolic navigation equipment and instrument landing systems.

You finish with a BTEC Certificate

Officer Careers

Officer entry is open to those who are over 18 and have at least 5 GCE O levels, including maths and English language. Many successful candidates have higher academic qualifications, and for some specialist branches a degree is required.

As well as aircrew — pilots and navigators — there are opportunities in branches such as Air Traffic Control, Engineering, Supply and Administration. Upper age limits vary from 23½ for pilots up to 39 for engineers.

Youth Training Scheme

It is also possible to join the RAF or the WRAF on the Youth Training Scheme. Further details from the RAF Careers Information Offices listed below.

Further Information

RAF Careers Information Offices:

Aberdeen: 63 Belmont Street, AB1 1JS
Aldergrove: RAF Aldergrove, Crumlin, Co Antrim
Ayr: 20 Wellington Square, KA7 1EZ
Bangor: The Drill Hall, Glynne Road, Gwynedd LL57 1AH
Bedford: 17 South Drive, Shortstown MK42 0UD
Birmingham: 14-16 Holloway Circus, B1 1BY
Blackpool: 10 Edward Street, FY1 1BA

Bournemouth: 244 Holdenhurst Road, BH8 8AS
Bradford: 33 Westgate, BD1 2QT
Brighton: 56 West Street, BN1 2RA
Bristol: Esso Building, 35 Colston Avenue, BS1 4TZ
Cambridge: 90 Regent Street, CB2 1DP
Canterbury: 17 St Peter's Street, CT1 2BJ
Cardiff: 109 St Mary Street, CF1 1PZ
Carlisle: 9 The Crescent, CA1 1QW
Chatham: 3 Dock Road, ME4 4FJ
Coventry: Broadgate House, Upper Precinct, CV1 1NU
Darlington: 148 Northgate, DL1 1QT
Derby: 35-36 Castlefields, Main Centre, DE1 2PE
Doncaster: 80 Cleveland Street, DN1 3DP
Dundee: 171 Overgate, DD1 1QF
Edinburgh: 21 Hanover Street, EH2 2DN
Exeter: Fountain House, Western Way, EX1 2DE
Glasgow: Charlotte House, 78 Queen's Street, G1 3DN
Gloucester: Lister Buildings, Station Road, GL1 1HE
Grimsby: 241 Freeman Street, DN32 9DW
Guildford: Steward House, Sydenham Road, GU1 3SR
Huddersfield: 26 Kirkgate, HD1 1QQ
Hull: 82-83 Prospect Street, HU2 8PE
Ilford: 180 Cranbrook Road, Greater London IG1 4LB
Inverness: 3 Bridge Street, IV1 1HG
Ipswich: 58 Princes Street, IP1 1RJ
Leeds: 10 Bond Court, LS1 2JY
Leicester: 84 Charles Street, LE1 1GH
Lincoln: 19-20 Saltergate, LN2 1DN
Liverpool: 53 London Road, L3 8HY
London: Kelvin House, Cleveland Street, W1P 6AU
Luton: 18-19 West Side Centre, off Dunstable Road, LU1 1ES
Manchester: Barnett House, 53 Fountain Street, M2 2AL
Middlesbrough: 69 Borough Road, TS1 3AD
Newcastle upon Tyne: 9 Ridley Place, NE1 8LP
Newport: 76 Sovereign Arcade, Kingsway Centre, NP1 1ED
Norwich: 6 Bridewell Alley, NR2 1AH
Nottingham: 70 Victoria Centre, Milton Street, NG1 3QX
Oldham: 70 Union Street, OL1 1DJ
Oxford: 35 St Giles, OX1 3LJ
Peterborough: 23 Hereward Centre, PE1 1TB
Plymouth: 69-73 Mayflower Street, PL1 1QR
Portsmouth: 11 Arundel Way, PO1 1NY
Preston: 83A Fishergate, PR1 2NJ
Reading: Liverpool Victoria House, Cheapside, RG1 7AH
St Helens: 7 George Street, WA10 1DA
Sheffield: 1 The Gallery, Castle Market Buildings, Exchange Street,
    S1 1FZ
Shrewsbury: 7–8 St Mary's Street, SY1 1EB
Southampton: 153 High Street, SO1 0BT
Southend: 524 London Road, Westcliff-on-Sea, SS0 9HS

Stoke-on-Trent: 36-38 Old Hall Street, Hanley, ST1 3PD
Sunderland: 4 Burdon Road, SR1 1QB
Swansea: 17-19 Castle Street, SA1 1JF
Swindon: 18 Milton Road, SN1 5JN
Taunton: 35 East Street, TA1 3LS
Truro: 107 Kenwyn Street, TR1 3DJ
Watford: 26 Station Road, WD2 5AF
Wolverhampton: 23 Victoria Street, WV1 3PD
Wrexham: 21 Rhosddu Road, LL11 1NF
York: 4 New Street, YO1 2RA

AUDIOLOGY TECHNICIAN

The work of the audiology technician involves giving hearing tests and providing and servicing hearing aids. Most audiology technicians are employed in National Health hospitals, but some work for local education authorities testing the hearing of schoolchildren.

To be admitted for training you should be 18 and have four O levels, including biology and physics. Apply to the Audiology Technicians Group of the British Society of Audiology.

Hearing aids are also dispensed privately. For particulars of registration and training as a private dispenser, consultant or practitioner you should contact the Hearing Aid Council or the Society of Hearing Aid Audiologists.

Further information

British Society of Audiology
Audiology Technicians Group
Harvest House
62 London Road
Reading
Berks RG1 5AS
0734 861345

BANKING

It is possible to go straight into banking from school with four O levels
and train on the job. In each bank some members of staff are given
the opportunity to train for a full career in banking, by being granted
study leave for the Institute of Banking examinations which are in
three stages. O level entrants study a two-year part-time BTEC National
Diploma in Business Studies as Stage 1. A level entrants study a one-
year Conversion Course as Stage 1. Successful completion of Stage 1
allows entry to Stage 2 which normally takes three years. For those
aspiring to senior management there is an official financial studies
diploma. In Scotland the Institute of Bankers in Scotland administers
the banking examinations.

Further information

Banking Information Service
Careers Section
10 Lombard Street
London EC3V 9AT
01-626 8486

Institute of Bankers in Scotland
20 Rutland Square
Edinburgh EH1 2DE
031-229 9869

Careers in Banking, Kogan Page

Where to look for jobs

Daily Telegraph
Guardian
Local press; most of the big banks advertise regularly

BEAUTY THERAPY

BEAUTY THERAPIST

The beauty therapist usually works in a salon, carrying out a wide range of treatments on the face and body. These include waxing, electrolysis, use of electronic instruments, Swedish massage and the use of vibrators and electronic devices for exercising muscles, manicure and pedicure. The therapist must be professionally trained. She can work either for the City and Guilds Certificate in Beauty Therapy (two-year full-time course) or for the Diploma of one of the professional bodies such as the International Health and Beauty Council. Three or four O levels are required for most courses and the minimum age is 18.

BEAUTY CONSULTANT

Works mostly in the cosmetics and perfumery departments of large stores, selling and demonstrating products and helping with beauty problems. Most of the large cosmetic firms run courses for sales consultants. Minimum age accepted is 18 and it is advisable to already have some selling experience. Professional training for the Beauty Consultant's Certificate requires two to three O levels.

Further information

Confederation of International Beauty Therapy and Cosmetology
Suite 5
Oriel Road
Cheltenham
Gloucestershire GL50 ITH
0242 570284

City and Guilds of London Institute
76 Portland Place
London W1N 4AA
01-580 3050

Institute of Electrolysis
251 Seymour Grove
Manchester M16 0DS

International Health and Beauty Council
UK Examinations Secretary
PO Box 36
Arundel
West Sussex BN18 0SW

International Therapy Examination Council
3 The Planes
Bridge Road
Chertsey
Surrey KT16 8LE
09328 66839

Northern Institute of Massage
100 Waterloo Road
Blackpool FY4 1AW
0253 403548

Careers in Hairdressing and
Beauty Therapy, Kogan Page

Where to look for jobs

Local press
Write to the big cosmetic firms asking if there are any openings
for trainees

BOOKKEEPER see Accountancy

BRICKLAYER see The Building Trade

BRITISH RAIL

British Rail is now one of the UK's largest employers, with a staff
approaching a quarter of a million. It has an enormous range of
employment, both on the railways themselves, whether as railman,
engineering technician or driver, in management, computer operations,
catering, and in other attendant businesses such as shipping,
hovercraft, hotels, property management and transport police.
However, *there is little recruitment at present* and applicants should
respond to advertised vacancies only.

JUNIOR RAILMAN

Entry is at 16-17 for school-leavers with a genuine interest in railway
operations. They are given general railway training and experience
within the Traffic Department, leading to responsible posts.

TRACTION TRAINEE

No qualifications required. Entry for school-leavers, preferably those who have studied maths and science. Training lasts for two to three years, while recruits are given training and experience in the driving cab to become driver's assistants and subsequently drivers (when over 21).

CRAFT APPRENTICE

Entry is 16-18 for school-leavers, preferably those with CSEs in maths and science and with an interest in practical work. They are given craft training within an engineering department and day- or block-release study for a craft certificate.

CLERICAL OFFICER

Entry is at 16-18 for school-leavers who have reached CSE or O level standard. The job involves clerical work in offices of all kinds, leading to administrative or management posts.

COMPUTER OPERATIONS

Entry is for school-leavers between 16 and 18 with at least two O levels, preferably in maths and English. Recruits are trained to become operations' assistants, leading through promotion to become computer operators or control clerks, with the opportunity to progress to more senior posts.

TRAINEE SIGNAL AND TELECOMMUNICATIONS TECHNICIAN

Entry is at 16-18 for school-leavers, preferably with O levels in maths and science, and with a genuine interest in practical work. Training lasts four years with either day- or block-release study for craft certificate.

ENGINEERING TECHNICIAN

Entry is for school-leavers aged 16-18. Must have O levels or equivalent in maths, English language and physics, or a combined science with physics. They are given a practical training course, lasting four years, in civil, mechanical and electrical engineering, or signal and telecommunications, combined with day- or block-release study for the appropriate Technician Certificate, leading to Higher Technician Certificate and senior technical posts.

QUANTITY SURVEYOR

Entrants must have four GCEs, three at A level, or five GCEs, two at A level, in subjects acceptable to the Royal Institute of Chartered Surveyors, as a preliminary to the first examination. Training is for membership of the RICS.

ENGINEERING SPONSORSHIP

British Rail sponsors degree courses in civil, mechanical, production, electrical (traction), electrical or electronic (signal and telecommunications) engineering. Students must have reached a level qualifying for university entrance for an honours degree course. Students take a sandwich course leading to an engineering degree and a career as railway engineering managers. Practical training is carried out in the engineering departments of the railway regions or in the works of British Rail Engineering Ltd.

FINANCE AND ACCOUNTANCY

Entrants must be under 21 and have or expect to have five GCEs, including maths and English, two at A level. They are trained over three to four years in railway financial work combined with sponsored study, by means of a sandwich course, for a professional accountancy qualification.

SUPPLIES MANAGEMENT

Entrants must have five GCEs, including English and maths, two at A level. Students take a sandwich course HND in Business Studies, combined with practical training in the work of the Supplies Department of the railways.

BRITISH TRANSPORT POLICE

Candidates with English and maths O levels are preferred.

GRADUATE ENTRY

Graduates with a relevant degree are taken on in estate management, computing, operating, marketing and personnel, retail and catering, finance and accountancy management, research and development and operational research.

Further information

British Railways Board
PO Box 100
Rail House
Euston Square
London NW1 2DZ
01-262 3232

British Rail Engineering Ltd
274-280 Bishopsgate
London EC2M 4XQ
01-247 5444

British Transport Police
15 Tavistock Place
London WC1H 9SJ
01-388 7541

London underground
as well as British Rail.

BRITISH TELECOM

British Telecom is responsible for providing, operating and maintaining inland and international telecommunications services. It also has large-scale computing and data processing operations. In order to run these services British Telecom employs about 230,000 staff with a wide range of skills.

CLERICAL AND EXECUTIVE STAFF

British Telecom has many clerical staff working in all its departments, including such areas as personnel, marketing and finance. There is a wide variety of work and in most cases staff have a high level of responsibility. The minimum entry qualification is two O levels or equivalent, or you may take an aptitude test to see whether you are suitable.

Those with at least five GCEs (two at A level) including English language, can join as executive officers, who are junior managers. Executive officers supervise clerical staff and carry out other managerial and administrative tasks.

ENGINEERING AND TECHNICAL STAFF

British Telecom is also a major employer of engineers and technicians. They are responsible for the design, research, development, provision and maintenance of all types of telecommunications equipment. Three-year apprenticeships are offered to young people under 18 with O levels or equivalent in science and maths, whilst those between 18 and 21 can be trained to be technicians under the Improver scheme. An apprenticeship scheme also exists for those interested in becoming motor mechanics to service the large fleet of British Telecom vehicles.

Each year a number of university studentships in engineering and science are offered to young people between the ages of 17 and 20 who have or are expected to get three good maths or science A levels. The students undertake a year of industrial training before entry to university and are paid a salary during their university course. Successful students are employed as engineering managers on graduation.

TELEPHONE STAFF

People with clear speaking voices who are tactful and enjoy talking to the public and helping them are employed as telephonists in telephone exchanges. Those with maths and science qualifications at A level can help in planning and forecasting the size of the communications systems needed for the future, as telecommunications traffic officers.

DATA PROCESSING STAFF

There are opportunities for O level holders to work as data processing operators, while those with five GCEs (two at A level) including English language, who show an aptitude for this kind of work, can be trained as programmers and systems analysts. All new entrants to data processing departments receive full training.

TYPING STAFF

With such a wide variety of administrative work, British Telecom needs many typing staff, who generally work in fairly small offices with a friendly and efficient atmosphere. Copy typists should have a typing speed of at least 30 wpm, shorthand-typists should be able to type at 30 wpm and write shorthand at 100 wpm and audio-typists must be able to type 30 wpm and transcribe a tape of 350 words in 30 minutes.

Further information

Vacancies vary according to local needs. Information about vacancies in your area and more details about opportunities in British Telecom can be obtained from the Personnel Department of your local telephone area, whose address and telephone number are in the front of your telephone directory.

Recruitment Publicity
CP2.2.2
81 Newgate Street
London EC1A 7AJ

THE BUILDING TRADE

Working in the building trade doesn't just mean using your muscles on a building site. It covers a wide range of crafts and skills, including carpenters, joiners, bricklayers, painters and decorators, crane drivers, electricians, plumbers, gas fitters, plasterers, glaziers, scaffolders, steel erectors, stone-masons, roofing and wall tilers, heating and ventilation specialists, which you can learn on the job as an apprentice. You obviously need to be fit and healthy, fairly practical and good with your hands.

The Construction Industry Training Board (CITB) runs courses at their training centre in Norfolk in earthmoving, construction, scaffolding and cranes, and at technical colleges in construction, earthmoving, cranes, scaffolding, building crafts (bricklaying and carpentry), tiling, painting and decorating, plumbing, etc. Many firms belong to the CITB training scheme and will be prepared to sponsor school-leavers. Under the present scheme trainees spend the first six months or so in full-time training, followed by two years' practical experience on the job combined with day-release training. The CITB may participate in the new Youth Training Scheme (not decided at time of going to press).

The earlier you start the better, as the *maximum* age for entry is usually 17. You will need a satisfactory school record and four medium grade CSEs. You will also be given a medical examination to make sure you are fit enough for the job. The CITB will help you find a sponsor (who then becomes your future employer) if necessary.

At technician level you can also do a two-year full-time college course leading to the BTEC or SCOTVEC Diploma in Building Studies. At this level, the entry qualifications are four O levels or CSE Grade 1 including maths, a science subject and English. If you want to start work straight away you can study part-time for the BTEC or SCOTVEC Certificate in Building Studies.

For the BTEC or SCOTVEC Higher Diploma in Buildings Studies you need an A level in maths or physics and four O levels including maths and physics. Courses are two years full-time or three years sandwich.

Further information

Construction Industry Training Board
Bircham Newton
King's Lynn
Norfolk PE31 6RH
048 523 291 (ext 213)

Jobs in Painting and Decorating, Kogan Page
Jobs in the Building Trade, Kogan Page

Where to look for jobs

Building (weekly)
Building Trades Journal (weekly)
Daily Telegraph
Local press

BUTCHER see Catering, The Meat Industry

CARPENTRY see The Building Trade

CARTOGRAPHY see Mapmaking

CATERING

Catering — providing food and/or drink services — is one of the largest industries in the UK, employing over one million people. You can work in a hotel, restaurant or cafe, large or small, or for an institution such as a school, hospital or factory. Remember that the work is often at unsocial hours.

There is always a demand for waitresses, barmen, kitchen helpers, etc and no qualifications are needed for these.

If you want to train for a professional career in catering, there are a great variety of routes you can take depending on which, if any, qualifications you have. For craft and unskilled operative jobs such as cook, waiter, room maid you could seek a job directly and attend college on a part-time basis, or go direct to college and study full-time. The craft courses available lead to a wide number of qualifications but the most important are offered by the City and Guilds of London Institute in the areas of cookery, food and beer services, housekeeping and accommodation services and reception. (In Scotland the hotel reception courses are administered by the Scottish Vocational Education Council (SCOTVEC)). Often students attending college on a full-time basis spend the first year doing a General Catering Course and then go on to specialise in a specific area. The academic requirements for these courses are minimal but they do vary from subject to subject.

For those who have better academic qualifications, for example four O level GCEs, they may prefer to attend college on a full-time basis and study for a BTEC or SCOTVEC Diploma in Hotel Catering and Institutional Operations. These courses last two years and are operated on a modular basis. At some colleges it is possible to study for a BTEC Certificate part-time. For those who want to go further at this stage it is possible to take the Hotel, Catering and Institutional Management Association's two-year part-time course, Part A of the HCI professional qualification.

For those with at least one A level it is possible to enrol directly for the BTEC or SCOTVEC Higher Diploma in Hotel, Catering and Institutional Management which takes three years of full-time study, usually including a period of industrial experience. The HCI Part B course is suitable for those who have either taken Part A or passed an OND, BTEC or SCOTVEC Diploma.

If you are interested in baking and have four O levels (including a science subject) you can take the National Diploma in Baking. You either do a two-year full-time course at a technical college or do part-time study while an apprentice, taking the City and Guilds Certificate.

51

Further information

Hotel and Catering Industry Training Board
Careers Information Service
PO Box 18
Ramsey House
Central Square
Wembley
Middlesex HA9 7AP
01-902 8865

Hotel, Catering and Institutional Management Association
191 Trinity Road
London SW17 7HN
01-672 4251

Institute of British Bakers
Regent House
Heaton Lane
Stockport SK4 1BS
061-477 4750

Careers in Catering and Hotel Management, Kogan Page
Jobs in Hotels, Kogan Page

Where to look for jobs

Catering Times (weekly)
Caterer and Hotelkeeper (weekly) for chefs, hotel staff, catering managers, etc
Dalton's Weekly
The Lady (weekly) for cooks/housekeepers
Local press, particularly evening papers

See also Home Economist, The Meat Industry

CHEMISTRY see Laboratory Technician, Pharmacy, Medical Laboratory Scientist

CHILDCARE see Nursery Nursing, Social Work

CHIROPODY

Chiropodists treat the many types of foot disorder and advise on all aspects of foot care. Applicants for training must have five GCE or SCE passes of which two must be A level or Highers in O level English and a science. Contact the Society of Chiropodists (for further information) for recognised schools or chiropody. The three-year training course is mainly practical. There are many opportunities for work, both in the National Health Service and in private practice.

Further information

Council for Professions Supplementary to Medicine
Park House
184 Kennington Park Road
London SE11 4BU
01-582 0866

The Society of Chiropodists
53 Welbeck Street
London W1M 7HE
01-486 3381

THE CIVIL SERVICE

The Civil Service is the single biggest employer in the country and employs staff at all levels, from clerks upwards. Its activities cover a wide area, from scientific research establishments and Social Security offices to the preservation of ancient monuments. If you find a job at your local Jobcentre the staff who help you will be civil servants; when you start paying National Insurance it is a civil servant who sends your card; and when you earn enough money to pay tax it is a civil servant who opens a file on you.

The Civil Service have a long-established system of training. At whatever level you enter, you will find a system of day-release and training schemes to encourage you to improve your qualifications and move up the promotion ladder.

53

CLERICAL ASSISTANTS

Every Civil Service department employs these assistants. They do routine filing and record-keeping and some simple figure work, perhaps using a calculator. They also deal with inquiries from the public. Entry qualifications are two O levels, including English language, or you take a test. You will be encouraged to take day-release classes to help you qualify for promotion to Clerical Officer.

TYPISTS AND SHORTHAND-TYPISTS

Office staff are needed in every department, doing normal office work. Typists should have 30 wpm and shorthand-typists 100 wpm. Staff are encouraged to take day-release classes to improve their skills and thus qualify for promotion.

PERSONAL SECRETARIES

Secretaries work for senior staff, up to Head of Department grade, and can hold highly responsible positions. Minimum age for entry is 18. Qualifications required are three O levels, including English, shorthand at 35 wpm and a typing speed of 100 wpm.

CLERICAL OFFICERS

Clerical officers are employed in all departments of the Civil Service. They deal with correspondence, including correspondence from the public, draft letters for senior staff, keep records and compile reports and statistics. From here, you can be promoted to Executive Officer. Entry qualifications are five O levels, including English (plus a foreign language for a Diplomatic Service post).

EXECUTIVE OFFICERS

Executive officers are the managers of the Civil Service. In some departments, such as the Inland Revenue or Customs and Excise, they work on individual cases which probably bring them into contact with the general public. Entry requirements from outside the service are two A levels and three O levels, including English, or two to three Scottish Highers. BTEC and SCOTVEC qualifications are accepted as alternatives. Promotion is also frequently made from Clerical Officer.

ASSISTANT SCIENTIFIC OFFICERS

A large number of scientists and engineers are employed in the 120 or so government research establishments which cover a wide field from nuclear research to conservation of resources. Entry qualifications are four O levels including English, a science and/or mathematical subject. As with other civil servants they are encouraged to study through day-release to improve their qualifications and thus gain promotion.

Specialist careers

MINISTRY OF DEFENCE TECHNICIAN APPRENTICES

Apprentices spend four years training in aeronautical, electrical, electronic, mechanical or metallurgical engineering or ship construction. The first year is spent in basic training. Apprentices then do a part-time day-release or block-release course at a technical college leading to a BTEC Certificate. Applicants should be under 19 with four O levels in maths, a science and English language.

CADET VALUERS

Valuers are employed by the Inland Revenue to value land and buildings for a variety of purposes, including the levying of rates and taxes, and purchases by government departments and local authorities.

DEPARTMENT OF THE ENVIRONMENT

There is a scheme for those with O level qualifications to train for a variety of technical appointments in the construction field. These normally include quantity surveying assistants, mechanical and electrical engineering technicians, and draughtsmen or women to work as architectural, civil engineering, electrical and heating and ventilating assistants. Applicants should be under 19 with four O levels including maths, physics or physics with chemistry and English language.

Further information

Civil Service Commission
Alencon Link
Basingstoke
Hampshire RG21 1JB
0256 29222

Careers in the Civil Service, Kogan Page

Where to look for jobs

Daily Telegraph
Guardian
Local press

CLERICAL WORK see Office Work, Secretarial Work

CLOTHING INDUSTRY see Fashion

COMPUTERS

COMPUTER OPERATORS

Operators are the people who actually run the computer, doing shift work. Most employers require four to five O levels or CSEs including maths and English. It is an advantage if you have taken Computer Studies at O or A level.

PROGRAMMERS

Programmers prepare the sequence of instructions (the computer program) that controls the computer. Qualifications required vary, depending on the specific job. For most jobs you would probably need a minimum of five O levels, including maths.

DATA PREPARATION

The data preparation operator uses a machine similar to a typewriter to transfer data into a form in which it can be read by the computer. A good general education to GCE/CSE standard is all that is required, but it is an advantage to be familiar with a typewriter.

TRAINING

There are various full- and part-time courses leading to BTEC and City and Guilds qualifications. Many companies also run their own training programmes.

You should consult a copy of *The Computer User's Handbook* at your local library for descriptions of jobs and courses available in computing.

Further information

The British Computer Society
13 Mansfield Street
London W1N 0BP
01-637 0471

Computer Service Industry Training Council (COSIT)
Fifth floor
Hanover House
73-74 High Holborn
London WC1V 6LE
01-242 5049

The Institute of Data Processing Management
50 Goschen Buildings
12 Henrietta Street
London WC2E 8NU
01-240 3305

National Computer Centre
Bracken House
Charles Street
Manchester M1 7BD

Careers in Computers and New Information Technology, Kogan Page

Where to look for jobs

Datalink (weekly)
Computing (weekly)
Computer Weekly
Daily Telegraph
Local press
Computer Talk (weekly)

COOKING see Catering, Home Economist

DECORATOR see The Building Trade

DENTAL WORK

DENTAL HYGIENIST

Hygienists teach patients oral hygiene, to scale and polish teeth and apply gum treatment under the direction of a registered dentist. For entry to a course, which lasts 9 to 12 months full-time, you must be 17 and have four O levels, including English language and at least one science subject. Courses are held at dental hospitals.

DENTAL SURGERY ASSISTANT

The assistant usually trains on the job, working beside the registered dentist. The job involves record-keeping, mixing fillings, handing instruments, helping with x-rays, etc. To enter for the National Examination you need at least 21 months' experience and two O levels or CSEs grade 1, including English language. There are also full-time and part-time training courses at the various dental hospitals.

DENTAL TECHNICIAN

Technicians are the craft workers who make and repair dentures, crowns and other appliances. They work either in commercial dental laboratories or in hospital laboratories. They train on the job, serving a five-year apprenticeship while preparing for the City and Guilds Dental Technician's Certificates. It is a highly skilled job which requires great manual dexterity. There are no entry qualifications.

Further information

Association of British Dental Surgery Assistants
DSA House
29 London Street
Fleetwood
Lancs FY7 6JY
03917 78631

British Dental Hygienists Association
64 Wimpole Street
London W1M 8AL
01-486 4856

General Dental Council
37 Wimpole Street
London W1M 8DQ
01-486 2171

The London Hospital Medical College
Dental Auxiliary School
Turner Street
London E1 2AD
01-377 8800

National Joint Council for the Craft of Dental Technician
64 Wimpole Street
London W1M 8AL
01-935 0875

Where to look for jobs

British Dental Journal (fortnightly)
Opportunities (weekly)
Community Care

DIETICIAN see Home Economist

DOMESTIC SCIENCE see Catering, Home Economist

DRAUGHTSMEN

Draughtsmen produce detailed drawings from which craftsmen produce the finished article — which can be anything from a machine part to a whole building. Neatness and accuracy are the most important skills. Many work in mechanical engineering, as well as electronic, civil, structural and aeronautical engineering. They also work in architecture and town planning.

Entry is through a craft or technician apprenticeship. Craft apprentices need no particular qualifications. Technician apprentices need four O levels or CSEs. Training is on the job by day- or block-release for the BTEC or SCOTVEC Certificates.

Further information

Council of Engineering Institutions
2 Little Smith Street
London SW1P 3DL
01-799 3912/4

The Society of Architectural and Associated Technicians
397 City Road
London EC1
01-278 2206

Where to look for jobs

Daily Telegraph
Municipal Journal (weekly)
Opportunities (weekly)

ELECTRICIAN see The Building Trade, Engineering

ENGINEERING

Engineering is a wide and varied field which offers many opportunities to young people of all interest and abilities. This includes women, who are now being actively encouraged to enter this field. There are many different kinds of engineering: civil, aeronautical, mechanical, electrical, electronic, production etc, and more than three million people are directly employed in engineering — most of them trained to operator, craftsman or technician level. In spite of the recession there are still opportunities for suitably qualified young people, but competition for apprenticeships is fierce.

THE OPERATOR

Operators do many different types of operational and assembly work, and perform important tasks at every stage of the production process. No formal school qualifications are required but, with more and more young people coming on to the job market with CSE and GCEs and the current shortage of vacancies in the industry, gaining acceptance by a local firm may be difficult without a good school report and some proficiency in maths, English, and a practical subject such as technical drawing, woodwork or metalwork.

Anyone over 16 can apply to train as an operator. Training may be given at the place of work or, on a day-release basis, at a local technical college. If you are successful at operator level and have the necessary GCEs and/or CSEs, it may be possible to go on to a City and Guilds or Regional Examining Board craftsman course.

THE CRAFTSMAN

There are more than half a million craftsmen in the engineering industry, skilled in several areas and working with relatively little supervision. Craftsmen, such as fitters, turners, welders and toolmakers, are important in mechanical and electrical engineering and in both production and maintenance.

Qualifications for an apprenticeship are usually three or four GCEs or good CSEs, in maths, physics, or another science, and English. Most apprenticeships will be started immediately on leaving school, ie at 16, and firms tend to prefer younger applicants.

Training is on a day- or block-release basis at the local technical college and is mainly practical. The apprenticeship lasts for three to four years. Training is off the job for the first year, while a wide range of trades are studied. On the job specialisation follows, and the apprentice trains in a specified trade. Depending on the speed with which you acquire the necessary skills and the needs of the sponsoring company, you may take another two or three years to attain the EITB Certificate of Engineering Craftsmanship.

Again, on successful completion of the course and if the sponsoring company is agreeable, the good trainee can then aim for technician status through a BTEC or SCOTVEC Certificate.

THE TECHNICIAN

There are some 200,000 technicians employed in engineering, and this group forms the link between professional engineers who design engineering systems and production processes and the operators and craftsmen who operate and maintain them. Technicians are important in research and development, testing, planning and supervising production. Many move into plant operation and general management. Applicants should have at least four GCEs or Grade 1 CSEs, including maths, another science (preferably physics), a practical subject and English. Most technicians are given apprenticeships by local firms who pay them while they take a BTEC or SCOTVEC Certificate through a day- or block-release course at the local technical college. Again, successful applicants for apprenticeshps will usually be 16 or 17.

Training lasts four years. The first year is off the job, working at a training centre. This provides the necessary framework for future study, but near the end of the course the trainee begins to prepare for his particular specialisation. On completion of the whole course of training the trainee receives a BTEC Certificate or Diploma. Most trained technicians enter industry through the firm to which they are apprenticed, though some may go on to study to a professional level.

Further information

Engineering Careers Information Service
54 Clarendon Road
Watford WD1 1LA
98 38441

Engineering Industry Training Board
PO Box 176
54 Clarendon Road
Watford WD1 1LA
98 38441

Business and Technician Education Council (BTEC)
Central House
Upper Woburn Place
London WC1H 0HH
01-388 3288

Scottish Vocational Education Council (SCOTVEC)
22 Great King Street
Edinburgh EH3 6QH
031-557 4555

Jobs in Engineering, Kogan Page

Where to look for jobs

Details of apprenticeships are available from your careers officer, local Jobcentre or employment office.

ESTATE AGENT

An estate agent is in effect a go-between, acting as a negotiator between the seller (the client) and prospective buyers. Estate agency covers a vast field of operation: residential houses, country estates, farms, shops, offices, industrial premises, overseas property, lettings and the sale of second-hand goods and valuables. Some agencies handle most of these categories, but many specialise in one or two areas.

You need a very strong personality to be a successful estate agent. You have to be tactful, yet firm, able to back your own judgement. You must not be easily discouraged, as the cancellation rate is enormous — a sale that you have put a lot of time and effort into can be cancelled overnight on a whim. You have to be adept at meeting and chatting with people, able to make a good impression and win their confidence. Buying and selling property — especially houses — can be a highly emotional and worrying business for those concerned, and the estate agent has to be able to cope with people who may be under a lot of stress. A good telephone manner is essential, and of course you must be able to write crisp, compelling sales literature.

Routine jobs involved include the measurement of property, placing of advertisements, preparation of details and window displays. You will also have to learn the mortgage market — the agency you join may have an active building society connection with funds regularly being invested and withdrawn by local people. Books and records must be kept accurately.

The progression is from junior negotiator to senior negotiator to branch manager.

Training

The College of Estate Management offer a one-year correspondence course which includes residential weekends. There are no entry qualifications. The Polytechnic of Central London also offers a one-year part-time certificate which involves two evening classes a week. Entry is O level standard.

If you want to become a qualified specialist, a number of organisations run training courses leading to qualification by examination. The Royal Institution of Chartered Surveyors, for example, requires a minimum of two A levels and five O levels and other professional bodies have similar entry requirements.

Further information

College of Estate Management
Whiteknights Park
Reading RG6 2AW
0734 861101

The Incorporated Society of Valuers and Auctioneers
3 Cadogan Gate
London SW1X 0AS
01-235 2282

The National Association of Estate Agents
Arbon House
21 Jury Street
Warwick CV34 4EH
0926 496800

Polytechnic of Central London
35 Marylebone Road
London NW1 5LS
01-486 5811

The Rating and Valuation Association
115 Ebury Street
London SW1W 9QT
01-730 7258

The Royal Institution of Chartered Surveyors
12 Great George Street
London SW1P 3AD
01-222 7000

EYE CARE

(including Optometrist or ophthalmic optician, dispensing
optician, orthoptist, ophthalmic nurse, optical technician,
clinical assistant, optical receptionist)

There is a variety of inter-connected jobs in the field of eye care, from
making of lenses and spectacle frames, to nursing, the orthoptist who

examines the eye and writes a prescription, to the technician who makes lenses and spectacle frames.

This is an area where qualifications range from degree course (for the optometrist) to none at all (for the receptionist).

OPTICAL RECEPTIONIST

The optical receptionist makes appointments for both optometrist and dispensing opticians and is usually the first person you have contact with if you go to have your eyes tested. They need some background knowledge and expertise to cope with minor problems, such as uncomfortable or badly fitting frames.

A course is available, one evening a week, at City and East London College, to give receptionists an insight into the profession and some practical skills. There are no special educational requirements for the course.

OPTOMETRIST (formerly known as ophthalmic optician)

It is the optometrist who examines your eyes and decides whether you need spectacles. Sometimes he then has to refer the patient to the GP or to a hospital on account of disease that has been detected as a result of his examination. He also writes the prescription for spectacles, if needed.

The optometrist may work on his own or as part of a team in a practice.

TRAINING

The basic course in optometry is a BSc degree (three years in England and Wales, four years in Scotland). Qualifications for entry to the course are two A levels, usually from physics, biology, zoology, chemistry, and maths, plus three O levels, including English, and physics, or physics with chemistry. In Scotland, three Highers, from biology, anatomy, physiology, physics, chemistry, maths, engineering, and two O grades including English and physics or a biological subject.

DISPENSING OPTICIAN

The dispensing optician fits and supplies spectacles and contact lenses from prescriptions supplied by the Optometrist, but does not examine eyes.

TRAINING

Entry for training is at O level standard.

For entry to a training course you need four O levels, including English and maths or physics. Students either do a two-year full-time course in London, Glasgow or Bradford or a three-year day-release course in London. There is also a three-year correspondence course organised by the Association of British Dispensing Opticians (address below) combined with suitable employment.

ORTHOPTIST

The orthoptist's work involves the detection and treatment of squints and other abnormalities of eye movement and co-ordination. As part of the ophthalmologist's team, the orthoptist works in a hospital or clinic. Many of the patients will be infants and children, since all children under three must be screened and early correction begun if necessary. Orthoptists often work also in baby clinics, and school clinics, and therefore a liking for children is fairly important.

TRAINING

Basic entry requirements are two A levels and five O levels, in Scotland three Highers and five O grades. The student does a three-year full-time course at one of 10 hospital training schools for the Diploma of the British Orthoptics Council.

OPHTHALMIC NURSING (See also NURSING)

Ophthalmic nursing is a specialist option following a general nursing course. The ophthalmic nurse is exclusively concerned with caring for patients with eye conditions either in a general or specialised hospital. This includes duties in the operating theatre, casualty and out-patient departments and on wards. There is also a tremendous need for ophthalmic nurses in the Third World where poor hygiene and insect-borne disease results in a high incidence of eye disorders and infections.

TRAINING

Once the general nursing training is completed (see NURSING) the nurse follows a course at one of the 19 hospitals offering training in this speciality. The training is organised by the Ophthalmic Nursing Board (address below).

OPTICAL TECHNICIAN

The optical industries cover a wide range of enterprises concerned with optical lenses, spectacle lenses, contact lenses, lenses for precision instruments such as cameras, telescopes etc, and the manufacture of spectacle frames.

Apart from specialist manufacturers of specialist optical and eye examination instruments, there are also some large firms concerned with producing spectacles or contact lenses on prescription.

TRAINING

Most technicians train 'on the job', having entered the optical industry straight from school. Qualifications vary, but O levels in science subjects is the minimum requirement. While gaining practical experience technicians take a two-year day-release course at City and East London College aimed at the Optical Technician's Certificate. There are also three to four day Modular Course Programmes which are organised all over the country. Both kinds of course are organised by the Worshipful Company of Spectacle Makers (address overleaf).

Further information

Association of British Dispensing Opticians
22 Nottingham Place
London W1M 4AT
01-935 7411

British Orthoptics Society
Tavistock House North
Tavistock Square
London WC1H 9HX
01-397 7992

City and East London College
Department of Applied Optics
Bunhill Row
London EC1 8LQ
01-628 0864

General Optical Council
41 Harley Street
London W1N 2DJ
01-580 3898

Moorfields Eye Hospital   (the major teaching hospital for
City Road   ophthalmologists, ophthalmic nurses
London EC1V 2PD   and orthoptists)
01-253 3411

The Ophthalmic Nursing Board
Moorfields Eye Hospital
City Road
London EC1V 2PD
01-253 3411

The Worshipful Company of Spectacle Makers
Apothecaries Hall
Black Friar's Lane
London EC4V·6EL
01-236 2932

Careers in Eye Care, Kogan Page

FARMING see Agriculture

FASHION

You can start at the bottom in a shop or a fashion workshop, literally picking up pins from the floor, or you can train through various college courses. The Clothing Institute has a two-part examination leading to its own qualification — the course is either a four-year sandwich course or a two-to-three-year full-time course. Five O levels are needed for entry. The City and Guilds Institute offers vocational qualifications which train students to work in light clothing manufacture or in bespoke or retail tailoring. There are also BTEC awards at all levels in clothing. Fuller information is provided in *Careers in Fashion*, Kogan Page.

DESIGNERS

They have to produce new ideas and designs for clothes. They are usually employed by wholesale fashion houses, though some work freelance. Various colleges run fashion design courses, for which you need five O levels.

PATTERN CUTTING

This is a highly technical job which involves translating the designer's sketch into a paper pattern which is then graded into various sizes. You can take a college course in fashion or a BTEC Diploma or Certificate — minimum qualification GCE/CSE standard.

FITTERS

In fashion workrooms they are often in charge, organising the work, meeting buyers and approving designs. In retail shops they are responsible for customer alterations.

MACHINISTS

They actually sew the garments once they have been designed and patterns cut. No qualifications are required.

MODELLING

This is a very popular job with a glamorous image, but it is a very competitive business. The best way in is to train at a reputable modelling school which may then help to place you with an agency. Fuller information is provided in *Careers in Modelling*, Kogan Page.

Further information

College for the Distributive Trades
Leicester Square
London WC2H 0DX
01-839 1547
(Specialises in retailing and merchandising in the fashion industry
and organises courses for shop assistants and buyers)

The Clothing and Allied Products Industry Training Board
Tower House
Merrion Way
Leeds LS2 8NY
0532 441331

The Clothing and Footwear Institute
71 Brushfield Street
London E1 6AA
01-247 1696

London College of Fashion
20 John Prince's Street
London W1M OBJ
01-493 8341

Textile Institue
10 Blackfriars Street
Manchester M3 5DR
061-834 8457

Jobs in the Textile and Clothing Industries, Kogan Page

Where to look for jobs

Daily Telegraph
Draper's Record (weekly)
Local press

THE FORESTRY COMMISSION

Half the forests in Great Britain are publicly owned, and the Forestry
Commission is responsible for planting, conserving and managing the
forests and marketing the produce. Forestry includes everything from
planting trees in Scotland to raising millions of seedlings in nurseries

to producing trees for streets and open spaces in towns and cities. It also involves felling and transporting timber to sawmills and pulp factories.

FOREST WORKERS

Forest workers are employed on a wide range of jobs including fencing, planting, training, weeding, pruning, cutting timber, nursery work, and they also have to operate machinery in the forest. Training is given on the job to enable the worker to qualify as a forest craftsman and there are opportunities for promotion to ganger and foreman. Forest protection and wild life conservation is carried out by rangers — vacancies are usually filled by forest workers who show an aptitude for this kind of work. No special entry qualifications are required, except physical fitness.

FORESTERS

Foresters are the forest managers, responsible for planning annual work programmes, supervising forest workers, estimating costs, controlling work programmes, protecting forests. They are also responsible for relations with neighbouring landowners, organisations and individuals who want to use the forest for sport or recreation.

The training centres for foresters are Cumbria College of Agriculture and Forestry where students take a three-year sandwich course leading to the BTEC National Diploma, and Inverness Technical College where students take a two-year sandwich course leading to a SCOTVEC Diploma in Forestry. Entry requirements for these courses are a minimum of four O levels or equivalents, of which two should be science subjects, and one showing a command of English. Students must have had at least two years' practical forestry experience before starting the course, and an offer of a place at a college will be provisional on gaining this experience. For students with an offer of a place, the Forestry Commission is prepared to consider applications for employment as forest workers.

If you have not applied or have not been accepted for a place at one of the above colleges you should apply to the local forest office (not the Forestry Commission) in the area in which you wish to work (see telephone directory).

Careers Working Outdoors published by Kogan Page is a useful source of information.

CARTOGRAPHIC STAFF

Cartographic staff draw maps for publication and display, as well as general work such as drawing graphs, diagrams and wall-charts. Entry qualifications are three O levels for cartographic draughtsman and two O levels for cartographic assistant. Vacancies are usually advertised locally.

CLERICAL STAFF

As with all government departments, the Forestry Commission employs clerical staff to handle correspondence, records and give information to the public. Entry qualifications for a Clerical Assistant are two O levels and for a Clerical Officer, five O levels. Vacancies are advertised in the local press and in Jobcentres.

Further information

The Forestry Commission
231 Corstorphine Road
Edinburgh EH12 7AT
031-334 0303

For further information about the Training Centre for Foresters write to:

Cumbria College of Agriculture and Forestry
Newton Rigg
Penrith
Cumbria
0768 63791

Careers Working Outdoors, Kogan Page

Where to look for jobs

Local press

GARDENING & HORTICULTURE

There are openings as gardeners in market gardening, fruit farming, garden centres, nurseries, with local authorities in their parks departments and with institutions such as hospitals in their grounds. This job means hard physical work and often long hours, especially in commercial nurseries. Much of the work, such as planting, thinning, picking, pruning, etc is done by hand.

No educational qualifications are needed, but if you want to train there is a wide range of courses available from CGLI level upwards. There is a national apprenticeship scheme, involving practical training and part-time classes, which is operated by employers together with the Agricultural Training Board. Write to the Board for details.

The Royal Botanic Gardens offer a Diploma after three years' practical
work at the Gardens. Candidates must be 19, with two years' experience,
and have four O levels including English and maths or science. The
School of the National Trust for Scotland runs a two-year full-time
course for students aged 17 - 20 with one year's practical experience.
The Royal Horticultural Society and Kew Gardens both run their own
Diploma schemes.

Places on horticultural units are available within the Youth Training
Scheme, and a year on YTS can count as the first year of an
apprenticeship, or serve as a pre-college year of practical training.
Ask your local Careers Officer for details.

Further information

Agricultural Training Board
Bourne House
32-34 Beckenham Road
Beckenham
Kent BR3 4PB

Good Gardeners Association
Arkley Manor
Arkley
Barnet
Herts
01-449 2177/3031

Horticultural Education Association
Careers Officer
Askham Bryan College
York YO2 3PR
0904 706232

The National Trust for Scotland
School of Gardening
Threave House
Castle Douglas
Kirkcudbrightshire
0556 2575

British Retail Florists Association
5 Bishopscote Road
Luton
Bedfordshire LU3 1NX
0582 597353

The Royal Botanic Garden
Edinburgh EH3 5LR
031-552 7171

The Royal Botanic Gardens
Kew
Richmond
Surrey TW9 3AB
01-940 1171

The Royal Horticultural Society
Vincent Square
Westminster
London SW1P 2PE
01-834 4333

Careers in Floristry and Retail Gardening, Kogan Page

Where to look for jobs

Dalton's Weekly
Opportunities (weekly) for local authority jobs
Local press

HAIRDRESSING

No special qualifications are needed to become a hairdresser, though you obviously need to be fit as you will be on your feet all day. There are three different ways of training: you can be apprenticed for three years to a salon approved by the British Hairdressing Council, studying part-time for the City and Guilds Certificate; or you can take a two-year full-time course at a technical college, leading also to the City and Guilds examination; or you can take a six to nine month course at a private hairdressing school. There are no particular entry qualifications for the college courses, except that students must be over 16 and have a good standard of education.

Further information

National Hairdressers' Federation
11 Goldington Road
Bedford MK40 3JY
0234 60332

Hairdressing Council
12 David House
45 High Street
London SE25 6HJ
01-771 6205

Incorporated Guild of Hairdressers
24 Woodbridge Road
Guildford
Surrey GU1 1DY
0483 67922

Careers in Hairdressing and Beauty Culture, Kogan Page

Where to look for jobs

Hairdressers' Journal (weekly)

HEATING ENGINEER see The Building Trade

HEALTH SERVICE ADMINISTRATION

Administrators in the Health Service are non-medical staff. They are responsible for the smooth running of the service and their jobs cover general and financial planning, personnel, forward planning, responsibility for the upkeep of buildings, catering, transport, purchase of supplies and equipment, laundry, etc. You need to be efficient, with good organising ability.

You will work in one of the Regional or District Health Authorities offices or in a hospital or health centre. Minimum educational qualification for entry is four O levels or CSE Grade 1, from school, college or university. There are a number of training schemes providing for entry at all levels. All these schemes have periods of practical and theoretical training followed by practical experience in responsible posts. Trainees are expected to study for appropriate professional qualifications and are given every encouragement to do so with grants, day-release and schemes for trainee officers to gain experience of different departments.

Further information

All Wales Personnel Committee
c/o HM2 Division
Room 2003
Welsh Office
Cathays Park
Cardiff CF1 3NQ
0222 825111

The Institute of Health Service Administrators
75 Portland Place
London W1N 4AN
01-580 5041

The National Staff Committee for Administrative and Clerical Staff
Department of Health and Social Security
Hannibal House
Elephant and Castle
London SE1 6TE
01-407 5522

Scottish Health Service
Common Services Agency
Management Education and Training Division
Crewe Road South
Edinburgh EH4 2LF
031-332 2335

Where to look for jobs

Daily Telegraph
Guardian
Opportunities (weekly)
Municipal Journal
Community Care

HEALTH VISITOR

The health visitor's main job is preventive medicine, educating people
in proper health care, visiting mothers with new babies and young
children and giving practical advice. They also visit people discharged
from hospital, elderly people, handicapped people and anyone else the
doctor or social worker may ask them to keep an eye on. Health
visitors also teach and advise school children and adults on health
care. They may work from doctors' practices or from health centres.

To become a health visitor you must first qualify as a SRN, obtain a
recognised obstetric or midwifery qualification and complete a one-year
course in college. Minimum qualifications required are five O levels.

Further information

The English National Board for Nursing, Midwifery
and Health Visiting
Careers Advisory Centre
26 Margaret Street
London W1N 7LB
01-631 0979; no personal visitors.

The Scottish National Board for Nursing,
Midwifery and Health Visiting
22 Queen Street
Edinburgh EH2 1JX
031-226 7371

Where to look for jobs

Health and Social Service Journal (weekly)
Opportunities (weekly)
Nursing Times and Nursing Mirror (weekly)

HOME ECONOMIST

Home economists work as advisers and demonstrators for manufacturers
of domestic equipment, for the various food marketing boards and for
the gas and electrical industries as well as in community work,
residential homes, with local councils, schools, hostels, clubs and
hospitals. They can also work freelance, for photographers, advertising
agencies and publishers who want food professionally prepared for
photography.

All jobs require training. There are many different courses available
at further education colleges including many practical ones but the
main ones are the BTEC Diploma in Home Economics, a two-year
course which you can begin at 16 if you have three O levels in
English, maths and a science, and the BTEC Higher Diploma in Home
Economics, a three-year course for which you have to be 18 or over
with one A level.

The City and Guilds of London Institute runs the Certificate in Home
Economics for Family and Community Care which is a full-time two-
year course specialising in home economics relevant to the caring of
others. There are no academic entry requirements but candidates must
be at least 16 years old. Employment opportunities in this field include

residential care of the elderly, young, or handicapped, occupational therapy, welfare assistance, mother's help and assistant houseparent.

The Cook's Professional Certificate run by City and Guilds can be studied for full- or part-time and is suitable for those who already have a sound knowledge of cookery. Employment opportunities include running directors' dining rooms, private receptions and small high class catering establishments.
See also: Catering

Further information

Institute of Home Economics
192-198 Vauxhall Bridge Road
London SW1V 1DX
01-821 6421

Institute of Home Help Organisers
11 Delves Close
Ringmer
Sussex
0273 812145

Careers in Home Economics, Kogan Page

Where to look for jobs

Caterer and Hotelkeeper (weekly)
The Lady (weekly) for housekeepers
Opportunities (weekly)

HORTICULTURE see Gardening

HOTEL INDUSTRY see Catering

INSURANCE

Insurance is a service industry. It provides financial security for commercial and industrial business of all sizes and also protects the individual against the risks of fire, burglary, accident, sickness or premature death. There are about 400 insurance companies in the UK, as well as insurance brokers, underwriting syndicates and Lloyd's of London, which is the world's leading insurance company. Within the industry there is a vast range of jobs open to you.

In a company you might be assigned to sales, underwriting or claims, while there are also opportunities in specialist areas such as loss adjusting, investment or actuarial work. In addition, there is a whole army of back-up support staff — secretarial, personnel, computer, accounts, legal etc. (For further information see *Careers in Insurance* published by Kogan Page.)

BROKING

An insurance broker places insurance on behalf of a client, which means acting as go-between client and insurer, deciding on the best policy and negotiating the best premium. If you are interested in joining, you should apply to firms belonging to the British Insurance Brokers' Association (BIBA) as they will be able to provide a thorough technical training and sufficient working experience.

Training

Brokers recruit O and A level school-leavers and graduates. Normally the minimum requirement is three to four O levels, but A levels are preferred. However, personal qualities are even more important; brokers look for extrovert people with a lot of self-confidence. In effect there is a two-tier entry system, as elsewhere in insurance. O level entrants are placed in less technical positions, in departments such as accounts and data processing. Training varies greatly from firm to firm and usually entails both training on the job and work for professional qualifications.

UNDERWRITERS

An underwriter is anyone who has the authority to insure someone, set the premium and issue the policy. Most underwriters are employed by insurance companies. Entry can be at O or A level.

Training

Training is mainly on the job, but is supplemented by general insurance courses. To progress, underwriters must work for the professional examinations of the Chartered Insurance Institute (CII). They can then choose whether to specialise or to move sideways to become sales inspectors or surveyors.

SURVEYING

The surveyor prepares reports and plans of the 'risks' for the underwriter to examine. Surveyors are usually recruited from qualified commercial underwriting staff with three years' underwriting experience. Alternatively, graduates may be recruited directly, if they have a relevant degree: in estate management, maths, sciences or engineering.

SALES

Selling is an important part of the insurance business. Some sales staff are employed directly by companies on a commission basis; others, such as brokers, sell insurance for commission. These agents form part of a sales team coordinated by inspectors. The inspector's main job is to generate new business for the branch. He or she must be able to communicate with people at all levels and be skilled at persuasion and negotiation. The sales department in the office provides clerical back-up and customer information services.

CLAIMS

The function of a claims department is to ensure the prompt and fair settlement of claims. The claims handler is the person who decides whether or not a claim is admissible under the terms of the policy and decides how much the company should pay.

Training

Recruits to a claims department will need a minimum of two A levels, though in some circumstances O level applicants may be accepted. Most recruits are placed on a general trainee programme before moving on to claims.

COMPANY TRAINING PROGRAMMES

Generally, there is a two-tier training programme. Recruits will either attend courses for technical trainees, designed primarily for A level entrants, or the general clerical training schemes designed for O level entrants. Courses for management and supervisory work are provided for people who reach the appropriate level.

Further information

The central educational and professional body is the Chartered Insurance Institute. Students work first for the associateship and then the fellowship of the Institute. The Institute offers correspondence study courses to prepare students for the examinations. Alternatively, various colleges of further education or polytechnics offer courses of study for the Institute's examinations.

The British Insurance Association
Aldermary House
10-15 Queen Street
London EC4N 1TU
01-248 4477

The British Insurance Brokers' Association
14 Bevis Marks
London EC3A 7NT
01-623 9043

Chartered Institute of Loss Adjusters
Mansfield House
378 Strand
London WC2R 0LR
01-836 6482

Chartered Insurance Institute
20 Aldermanbury
London EC2V 7HY
01-606 3835

Chartered Insurance Institute Tuition Service
31 Hillcrest Road
London E18 2JP
01-989 8486

Corporation of Lloyd's
Lime Street
London EC3M 7HA
01-623 7100

The Faculty of Actuaries
23 St Andrew Square
Edinburgh EH2 1AQ
031-556 6791

The Institute of Actuaries
Staple Inn Hall
High Holborn
London WC1V 7QJ
01-242 0106

Insurance Institute of London
20 Aldermanbury
London EC2V 7HY
01-606 3763

The Pensions Management Institute Ltd
PMI House
124 Middlesex Street
London E1 7HY
01-247 0901

The Society of Investment Analysts
211 High Street
Bromley BR1 1NY
01-464 0811

LABORATORY TECHNICIAN

Laboratory technicians are employed in a wide variety of jobs. In industry they assist in testing and developing new products — foodstuffs, drugs, cosmetics, plastics, etc. They are employed in the medical and science departments of universities, helping with research projects and preparing material for lectures; they are also responsible for the care and maintenance of apparatus used in experiments. Technicians are employed by the scientific branch of the Civil Service — where they are called Assistant Scientific Officers — in government-run research establishments which cover a wide range of projects from nuclear defence to long-range weather forecasting. In hospitals, technicians work under the supervision of medical staff, operating the growing battery of equipment such as heart-lung machines, electroencephalograph machines, cardiographs, life-support systems used in intensive care units, etc.

Training is usually done on day- or block-release while in a job. For entry to training you need four O levels, two of them in scientific subjects. You then study for the ONC and HNC in Science. For BTEC and SCOTVEC awards entry qualifications can be lower. For the Science Laboratory Technician's Certificate, awarded by the City and Guilds of London Institute, you need three O levels, two of which must be science subjects. Training is again by day- or block-release.

See also Animal technician; Medical laboratory scientist

Further information

Institute of Science and Technology
Staple Inn Buildings South
335 High Holborn
London WC1V 7PX
01-405 9443

Where to look for jobs

Daily Telegraph
Opportunities (weekly)
Local press

THE LAW

LEGAL EXECUTIVE

The legal executive works in a solicitor's office, helping with the paperwork, looking up references, liaising with clients and preparing documents. Training is done on the job, attending day-release or evening classes to prepare for the exams of the Institute of Legal Executives. Normal entry qualifications for training are four academic O levels, but it may be possible to go into an office as a clerk with lower qualifications and acquire the necessary O levels at evening classes.

Further information

The Institute of Legal Executives
Kempston Manor
Kempston
Bedford MK42 7AB
0234 857711

BARRISTER'S CLERK

Clerks organise the work of the barrister's office (Chambers) and are responsible for its smooth running. The work of the junior clerk is very much that of the office-boy: making tea, running errands, etc but the senior clerks have a great deal of power and responsibility, negotiating fees and often deciding which barrister is to be given which brief (legal case). Entry qualifications are three O levels including English.

Further information

Barristers' Clerks Association
Lamb Building
Temple
London EC4Y 7AS
01-353 6701

Careers in the Law, Kogan Page

Where to look for jobs

Daily Telegraph
Municipal Journal
Journal of the Institute of Legal Executives
Local press

LIBRARY ASSISTANT

To train as a librarian proper you need two A levels and three O levels, including English language. However, it is possible to get a job as a library assistant with much lower qualifications, though there is no prospect of advancement. There is a one-year day-release course leading to a City and Guilds Certificate, for which you must have two years' experience in a library. Alternatively, with four O levels you can take the BTEC National Certificate in Library and Information Work, studying for two years part-time whilst working in a library. With this you can go on to take the professional library examinations.

Students who would like eventually to have better prospects could work as an assistant for a few years while they get the necessary A levels and then apply for a grant to take the two-year course at a library school leading to the professional examination of the Library Association.

Further information

The Library Association
7 Ridgmount Street
London WC1E 7AE
01-636 7543

Careers in Librarianship and Information Science, Kogan Page

Where to look for jobs

Local press

LOCAL GOVERNMENT

A job in local government can mean working in education, libraries museums, town and country planning, environmental health, housing, transport planning, waste disposal, police and fire services, parks and leisure facilities and all the social services. Local government employs all sorts of professional people — architects, librarians, social workers, accountants — as well as general clerical, administrative, manual, craft and managerial staff.

Clerical staff will probably have four O levels including English language, and for some jobs you may need secretarial qualifications. All staff are encouraged to work for higher qualifications. For jobs as draughtsmen or technician you need four O levels including maths. For jobs at administrative level you may need up to two A levels.

Some work demands no qualifications at all. Training will be given and often the opportunity to gain qualifications, for example in the case of highways and park employees doing manual work. Also craft apprenticeships are available for those with minimal qualifications.

Further information

Your local council is the best place to start.

Local Government Training Board
Arndale House, 4th Floor
The Arndale Centre
Luton LU1 2TS
0582 451166

The Employer's Secretary
Scottish Council
6 Coates Crescent
Edinburgh EH3 7AL

Careers in Local Government, Kogan Page
Jobs in Local Authorities, Kogan Page

Where to look for jobs

Daily Telegraph
Guardian
Municipal Journal (weekly)
Opportunities (weekly)
Local Government Chronicle
Professional Administration (weekly)
Local press

MAPMAKING

The Ordnance Survey takes on new recruits between 16 and 24, with a minimum of three GCE O levels or CSE Grade 1. Three of the subjects must include: English language, maths, geography, art, technical drawing, a science subject, a language, surveying. New surveyors take a nine-month training course at Southampton; new draughtsmen take a four-month training course at the Drawing School at Southampton.

Cartographic assistants carry out the simpler drawing connected with maps and plans: entry requirement is two GCE O levels or CSE Grade 1. For reproduction craftsmen a good education to GCE or CSE level is required, preferably with passes in maths, English, science or art. Candidates should be between 16 and 18. New entrants will take a City and Guilds craft course, involving one year full-time college study.

Further information

Ordnance Survey
Romsey Road
Maybush
Southampton SO9 4DH
0703 775555

Only those who have the minimum entry qualifications should apply.

See also Draughtsmen

THE MEAT INDUSTRY

The meat industry employs about 145,000 people who work in abattoirs and factories slaughtering and processing the meat we eat every day. They produce fresh meat in the form of chops, steaks, or joints, and processed meat like sausages, pies and hamburgers. This is distributed to shops and supermarkets all over the country, which employ many thousands more people.

The meat industry is large. For example, in Great Britain we consume annually over 3½ million tons of meat from this country and overseas.

THE ABATTOIR

Animals are killed and meat is prepared in large, modern factories similar to those operated by other industries. In fact, the same technology that has been applied to the production operation in other industries is now applied to abattoir operations.

You can be trained in abattoir skills such as those required for slaughtering animals and preparing them for sale. If you have the appropriate scientific qualifications you can become a meat technologist or an official meat inspector supervising standards of quality and hygiene.

There are many management opportunities in large abattoirs, and the managers of many large plants have 'worked their way up' through every stage of production.

THE WHOLESALER

The wholesaler is the link between the abattoir, the meat processor (or manufacturer) and the butcher or retailer. He buys meat in quantity from producers at home and overseas, securing the keenest price possible, then sells it in smaller lots, which provides a service to smaller businesses. Wholesalers have to know the trade thoroughly; a great deal of skill and knowledge has to be acquired to ensure that the meat is prepared in the best possible way, and is then handled efficiently and stored correctly.

MEAT MANUFACTURE

A great deal of our meat is eaten in the form of sausages, bacon, pies, canned meat and other manufactured products. In the industry this is known as meat manufacture and considerable craft skill is required in the preparation of the meat and in the production of meat products that the housewife will want to buy.

Meat manufacture is carried out in large, modern factories. Many job opportunities exist, ranging from general management to laboratory work and administrative and financial activities. Meat has also to be bought and sold, which provides other career opportunities in buying and selling.

THE BUTCHER

The representative of the meat trade who is best known to the public is the butcher — a highly skilled craftsman and trader. Young people starting as trainees or apprentice butchers are trained to develop skills in cutting carcases of meat into different joints; in handling all kinds of meat in a hygienic way; and, depending on the business, in helping their customers to choose the meat they buy.

To be a butcher you need to be healthy, neat and clean, and to have a keen eye and a steady hand. You will also need to be able to get up to start work early in the morning!

There are very good prospects for young people in butchery. You will be able to acquire skills and knowledge in a long-established craft, and find satisfaction in using them. You may also be able, if you have the flair, to own your own shop in time.

Training

The necessary entry qualifications to the industry depend entirely upon the nature of the job you will do or the skill you wish to acquire. You can start with an apprenticeship, and work your way up via part-time study at college. While it may not be necessary to have an educational certificate from school or college for entry to some jobs, the better the qualification the better your job prospects, particularly in the case of management trainees.

Some companies encourage their employees to obtain additional qualifications. They allow them time off to attend college courses and to sit for examinations administered by the Institute of Meat and other professional bodies. These courses are run at various colleges of further education up and down the country. They lead to affiliateship, associateship and eventually to membership of the Institute of Meat, and to the appropriate award of other professional organisations.

Further information

The Institute of Meat
Third Floor
56-60 John Street
London EC1M 4DT
01-253 2971

Smithfield Department of Food Technology
Briset House
6-9 Briset Street
London EC1M 5SL
01-253 7388

Where to look for jobs

Local press

MECHANIC see Engineering

MEDICAL LABORATORY SCIENTIST

Medical laboratory scientists work in hospitals, universities, public health laboratories and pharmaceutical firms, assisting in the diagnosis and treatment of diseases and research into the causes of disease.

For entry to training you must have at least four O levels, of which at least two must be biology and chemistry and one must indicate a good command of English. Training is on the job, studying part-time for the BTEC Certificate in Science (medical laboratory sciences) and the BTEC Higher Certificate in Medical Laboratory Sciences. Students with two A level passes in certain science and/or mathematical

subjects including biology and chemistry can enrol directly for the
part-time BTEC Higher Certificate course. *See also* Animal technician;
Laboratory technician.

Further information

Council for Professions Supplementary to Medicine
Park House
184 Kennington Park Road
London SE11 4BU
01-582 0866

Institute of Medical Laboratory Sciences
12 Queen Anne Street
London W1M 0AU
01-636 8192

Where to look for jobs

The Gazette of the Institute of Medical Laboratory Sciences (monthly)
Daily Telegraph
Opportunities (weekly)

MEDICAL SECRETARY

The medical secretary works in a hospital, or in a group practice or
health centre, or for an individual doctor, either GP or consultant. As
well as dealing with day-to-day correspondence the job involves a lot of
record-keeping, filing and administration. If you are working for a GP
or a consultant you will have more contact with patients, and tact,
patience and a friendly manner are essential here.

TRAINING

There are both full-time and part-time courses leading to the Certificate
in Medical Reception. For school-leavers with two O levels including
English language there is a one-year full-time course. The Diploma for
Medical Secretaries is a two-year full-time course for which you need
four O levels, one of which must be English language. You can then go
on to take the Diploma in Practice Administration. All these courses
are approved by the British Medical Association.

Further information

Association of Medical Secretaries, Practice Administrators
and Receptionists (AMSPAR)
Tavistock House North
Tavistock Square
London WC1H 9LN
01-388 2648

MERCHANT NAVY

DECK OFFICERS

These usually begin between 16 and 19 as deck cadets with a shipping
company. Schemes of training (sandwich) lead to the ONC or OND
in Nautical Science. The ONC in Nautical Science requires four O levels
for entry, including maths or physics. Cadets must pass the Department
of Trade sight test without glasses.

ENGINEER OFFICERS

These usually train through the Engineer Cadet Training Scheme, but
candidates who have completed a craft apprenticeship in a heavy
engineering workshop may also be appointed Junior Engineer Officers.
There are three courses of four-year sandwich training for engineer
cadets: the City and Guilds Marine Engineering Technician's Course
for which you must be at least 16, have completed secondary schooling
and completed the first year of a general course in engineering; OND in
Engineering for which you need four O levels; HND in Mechanical
Engineering (Marine) for which you need five GCEs including maths
and physics, one at A level.

RADIO OFFICERS

These have to obtain the Home Office Maritime Radiocommunications
General Certificate before going to sea. Candidates who obtain the
CGLI Certificate are exempt from Part I of the Examination. Entry
requirements are O levels in English, maths and physics. Most
employers also require the Department of Trade Radar Maintenance
Certificate.

DECK RATINGS

Admission is restricted to boys between 16 and 17½ who are selected
for pre-sea training by the industry and those over 18 with sea service.
For pre-sea training schools and colleges, see *British Qualifications.*

SHIPS' COOKS

Normal age for admission to the Merchant Navy is between 16 and 17½. Candidates must pass an exam at a School of Nautical Cookery approved by the Department of Trade. See *British Qualifications* for approved schools of cookery.

Careers at Sea published by Kogan Page is a useful source of information.

Further information (and lists of nautical engineering and radio colleges)

Merchant Navy Training Board
30-32 St Mary Axe
London EC3A 8ET
01-283 2922

MOTORBIKE MESSENGER

As the postal charges have gone up, and traffic becomes more and more congested, the messenger business has boomed. More and more firms now rely on motorbike messengers to deliver urgent letters, documents and parcels — the messenger can deliver in hours where the post might take several days.

To be taken on as a messenger you must own your own bike (250 cc), have a clean licence, and have a good knowledge of your city or town. Some firms ask for one year's previous experience before they will take you on. Messengers are self-employed — the firm pays 40p-60p a mile, but the messenger pays for his petrol, insurance etc, so it obviously pays to know your way about. A good messenger can earn £250 a week on average.

Where to look for jobs

For firms in your area look in Yellow Pages under 'Delivery and Collection'
Local press

NURSERY NURSING

Nursery nurses look after babies and young children under seven. Obviously you have to like children and enjoy being with them. You also need lots of energy, a good sense of humour, and endless patience and tolerance. You can work in a wide variety of situations — day nurseries run by the local authority, residential nurseries for children in care, hospitals and private homes.

Training

Minimum age for training is 16. Most courses are run in local Colleges of Further Education and last for two years, leading to the Certificate of the National Nursery Examination Board. Most of these colleges require a minimum of two O levels. Students spend two-fifths of the course working with children and three-fifths at college.

There are also four private training colleges (see further information) which are fee-paying. Minimum age for these colleges is 18.

Further information

Chiltern Nursery Training College
20 & 32 Peppard Road
Caversham
Reading
Berkshire
0734 471847

London Montessori Centre
18 Balderton Street
London W1
01-493 0165

National Nursery Examination Board
Argyle House
29-31 Euston Road
London NW1 2SD
01-837 5458
(You must send a stamped self-addressed envelope.)

Norland Nursery Training College
Denford Park
Hungerford
Berkshire
0488 82252

The Princess Christian College
26 Wilbraham Road
Fallowfield
Manchester M14 6JX
061-224 4560

Scottish Nursery Nurses Examination Board
38 Queen Street
Glasgow G1 3DY
041-204 2271
(You must send a stamped self-addressed envelope.)

Where to look for jobs

The Lady (weekly)
Opportunities (weekly)
Community Care (weekly)
Nursery World (weekly)

NURSING

Nursing requires not only compassion and a concern for people but also
a practical, down-to-earth approach to problems. You need to have a
strong sense of responsibility and the ability to take orders. Once
trained, you can specialise for example in care of the elderly or
mentally ill or you could move into community nursing outside the
hospital, for example; as a health visitor, district nurse or school nurse.
The Nurses Central Clearing House deals with all applications for basic
nurse training courses starting after 1 September 1987; application
should be made after one's seventeenth birthday.

ENROLLED NURSE (GENERAL) (EN)(G)

This is a two-year full-time course (18 months in Scotland) consisting
primarily of work on the wards under the supervision of qualified staff.
The age of entry is 18 in England and Wales (17½ in Scotland and
Northern Ireland). Most schools of nursing now ask for a minimum of
two O levels or equivalent to include English language or set an
entrance test. Pupil nurses (ie trainee RGNs) who wish to train for
mental nursing undertake a different course and qualify as a Registered
Mental Nurse (RMN) or as a Registered Nurse for the Mentally
Handicapped (RNMH).

REGISTERED GENERAL NURSE (RGN)

This full-time three-year training programme for student nurses (trainee RGNs) involves theoretical training and participation in the daily routine of all major wards and areas within the hospitals, and can involve work in such areas as psychiatry, obstetrics, care of the elderly, children's nursing, community experience etc. Schools of nursing now insist on applicants for registration training holding a minimum of five O levels, SCEs or CSE grade 1 passes. Most schools of nursing ask that these subjects are academic and some specify they should be obtained in one sitting. The very popular schools of nursing quite frequently give preference to A level candidates. The age of entry is 18 years (17½ in Scotland and Northern Ireland).

REGISTERED MENTAL NURSE (RMN) AND REGISTERED NURSE FOR THE MENTALLY HANDICAPPED (RNMH)

These two training programmes also last three years full-time and offer experience in the care of the mentally ill or mentally handicapped. Experience is gained in a wide range of settings both in the hospitals and in the community. Most schools of nursing ask for four or five O levels (usually academic) for these training programmes.

REGISTERED SICK CHILDREN'S NURSE (RSCN)

Training is undertaken either by doing a combined RGN/RSCN training lasting three years and eight months, or by undertaking an RGN training first and then following this with a post-registration course lasting 56 weeks. Competition for entry to the combined course is extremely fierce and academic requirements are likely to be well above the normal five O levels.

Further information

English National Board for Nursing, Midwifery and Health Visiting, Careers Advisory Centre, 26 Margaret Street, London W1N 7LB; 01-631 0979

Scottish National Board for Nursing, Midwifery and Health Visiting, 22 Queen Street, Edinburgh EH2 1JX; 031-226 7371

Welsh National Board for Nursing, Midwifery and Health Visiting, Pearl Assurance House, Greyfriars Road, Cardiff CF1 3RT; 0222 395535

The nursing officer of local regional health authorities (area health boards in Scotland)

Careers in Nursing and Allied Professions, 3rd edition, Kogan Page

Where to look for jobs

Community Care

Nursing Times and Nursing Mirror (weekly)
(These normally carry adverts for qualified staff only.)

See also The Armed Forces; Audiology Technician; Chiropody; Dental
Work; Eye Care; Health Service Administration; Health Visitor; Medical
Laboratory Scientist; Medical Secretary; Nursery Nursing; Occupational
Therapy; Physiotherapy; Social Work

OCCUPATIONAL THERAPY

Occupational therapists devise activities of all kinds to help patients
recover and regain their confidence. A calm, cheerful temperament is
needed, for as well as working in hospitals therapists are also employed
in institutions for the elderly and the mentally handicapped.
Occupational therapy is developing; there is now less emphasis on craft
activities and more on work involving thought and dexterity. Work
involving the mentally handicapped may have to be to some degree
repetitive and unchallenging, but it is now realised that other groups
(particularly psychiatric patients) should be given more responsibility
and greater scope for creativity and self-discipline. There is now more
emphasis on art and design, constructive group activities and on complex
manual tasks. For entry to a training course you must be 18 and have
six GCEs, one at A level.

Further information

The College of Occupational Therapists
20 Rede Place
London W2 4TU
01-229 9738

Council for Professions Supplementary to Medicine
Park House
184 Kennington Park Road
London SE11 4BU
01-582 0866

OFFICE WORK

CLERICAL WORK

Clerks handle all the paperwork involved in running any sort of business or institution. They receive and send letters, process forms and orders and file papers. Clerical work is carried out in all industrial and commercial firms and other institutions. It is not necessary to be able to type, only to have a good basic education to GCE/CSE standard. Many clerks are employed by the Civil Service and in local government.

Those who want to improve their qualifications can study part-time for BTEC Certificates. The Civil Service has its own examination structure for those who want to climb the promotion ladder.

OFFICE MACHINES

Increasing use is being made of machines in offices to simplify and speed up the flow of work. Many firms are prepared to train staff in the use of telex machines, information processors, calculating machines and word processors and will take on school-leavers who are willing to be trained. Pitmans offer a qualification in Word Processing — Theory and Practice. They also offer a Practical Word Processing Endorsement for those who have taken (or expect to take) the Intermediate or Advanced Typewriting Exam.

Further information

Business and Technician Education Council (BTEC)
Central House
Upper Woburn Place
London WC1H 0HE
01-388 3288

The Civil Service Commission
Alencon Link
Basingstoke
Hants RG21 1JB
0256 29222

Pitman Examinations Institute
Catteshall Manor
Godalming
Surrey GU7 1UU
04868 5311

Where to look for jobs

Daily Telegraph
Dalton's Weekly
Opportunities (weekly) for public service jobs
Local press, particularly evening papers

OPTICIANS (DISPENSING) see Eye Care

PAINTER see The Building Trade

PHARMACY

Dispensary technicians work under the supervision of qualified pharmacists, helping to make up prescriptions. They work in hospitals or in retail chemists' shops where part of the job is being a shop assistant as in any other shop, or in the pharmaceutical industry.

To enter for training you must have three GCE/CSEs Grade 1, including mathematics, English, biology or human biology and chemistry with physics or a similar subject. Training is done on the job, with two years' day-release or evening classes at college. (If your chemistry qualification is not good enough, you can take that subject first at evening class.)

A certificate is awarded by the Society of Apothecaries and by BTEC after a further year's study.

Further information

Pharmaceutical Society of Great Britain
1 Lambeth High Street
London SE1 7JN
01-735 9141

Scottish Department:
36 York Place
Edinburgh EH1 3HU

Pharmacy Assistants Training Board
The National Pharmaceutical Association
Mallinson House
40-42 St Peter's Street
St Albans
Herts AL1 3NP
0727 32161

Society of Apothecaries of London
Black Friars Lane
London EC4V 6EJ
01-236 1189

Careers in Pharmacy, Kogan Page

Where to look for jobs

Chemist and Druggist (weekly)
Pharmaceutical Journal (weekly)

PHYSIOTHERAPY

Physiotherapy is the use of physical means (exercise, manipulation and assistance in the use of specialist exercise machinery) to prevent injury and disease and to assist rehabilitation after illness. Physiotherapists treat all kinds of complaints and patients of all ages. They work in hospitals, rehabilitation centres, special schools for handicapped children, in sport, industry and in private practice.

Entry requirements are five O levels plus two A levels or three Scottish Highers, including English and two science subjects. Physiotherapists take a three-year full-time training course at a hospital or registered training school, leading to the qualification of Member of the Chartered Society of Physiotherapy.

Further information

The Chartered Society of Physiotherapy
14 Bedford Row
London WC1R 4ED
01-242 1941

Council for Professions Supplementary to Medicine
Park House
184 Kennington Park Road
London SE11 4BU
01-582 0866

PLUMBING see The Building Trade

THE POLICE

Policemen (and women) need to have good health, a liking for being outdoors whatever the weather, and the ability to work as one of a team. After a probationary two years on the beat you may have the opportunity to apply to specialise in traffic work, river police, mounted police, dog-handling, Special Branch, CID (including the Fraud Squad, Drug Squad and Regional Crime Squad).

Police cadets enter between 16 and 18, otherwise the minimum age for the police proper is 18½. Minimum height for men is 5ft 8ins and for women 5ft 4ins (many forces have higher standards). Physical fitness is essential. There are no specific educational requirements, but applicants take an entrance exam which includes English and maths. This may be waived for entrants with certain O level or CSE passes or if you have a degree.

Each of the 43 forces in England and Wales, the eight forces in Scotland and the one in Northern Ireland recruits independently. There is no central clearing house for applications. You should write for an application form to the chief officer of the force you would like to join.

Further information

Metropolitan Police
Careers Information and Selection Centre
6 Harrow Road
London W2 1XH
01-725 4212

Police Recruiting Department
Room 629
Home Office
50 Queen Anne's Gate
London SW1H 9AT
01-213 4074

The Job Finder's Book

Police Division
Scottish Home and Health Department
St Andrew's House
Edinburgh EH1 3DE
031-556 5601

Careers in the Police Force, Kogan Page

THE POST OFFICE

The size and scope of the Post Office offer opportunities for a large
range of careers carrying high rewards for achievement and responsibility.
The postal business is a major force in the country's communications
network. The 180,000 staff ensure that more than 30 million letters
and parcels are delivered every working day through a national system
of sorting offices; they run some 23,000 counters and 25,000 vehicles,
providing a complex range of postal, banking, licensing and other
services.

Recruitment of non-graduate staff is mainly carried out at local level.
Graduates should apply to their careers offices for information.

POSTAL CADETS

Open to young people aged between 16 and 18. No formal qualifications
are needed, only initiative and the ability to pass a simple aptitude test.
The work includes the collection and delivery of datapost, messenger
work, indoor sorting and outdoor delivery of telegrams. At 18, cadets
can become adult postmen/women with extra pay to match extra
responsibility, and a wider range of duties. Postal cadets work with
people their own age so that have the chance to make plenty of new
friends. Full training is given and uniforms are supplied.

POSTAL ASSISTANT

These posts are open to applicants aged 16 years and over. Selection is
by test and interview. Postal assistants are employed at the various
regional headquarters and at Postal Headquarters in London; also at the
Postal Finance Department in Chesterfield and some larger Head Post
Offices throughout the country. They are responsible for clerical work
such as sorting and filing papers, maintaining records, answering the
telephone and generally assisting postal officers and postal executives
with many different types of work. There are opportunities for
promotion to postal officer through an aptitude test and interview or
by obtaining the necessary educational qualifications.

POSTAL OFFICERS

Open to applicants aged 16 or over. Candidates should preferably have passes in GCE O level or CSE Grade 1 in English language and four other subjects (only three if one of the subjects is mathematics), although people without these qualifications will be considered provided they pass an aptitude test. All candidates must pass a formal interview. (All candidates in the London Postal Region must sit the aptitude test.)

Postal officers are vital links in the daily affairs of millions of people, as they serve behind Post Office counters, dealing with parcels, stamps, telegrams, pensions, licences and many other transactions. They may also work behind the scenes in an administration department dealing with such items as mails and postal service organisation, stock control, correspondence with the public, accounts, marketing, personnel, buildings management, etc.

Postal officers are fully trained for the varied work for which they will be responsible. Most recruits work initially at the counter and therefore spend their first weeks at one of the many counter training offices.

For counter staff the working week is spread over five days and the day off is often taken during the week, as post offices need to open on Saturdays. In the administrative office it is a five-day week from Monday to Friday. You work a 42-hour (41 hours in London) week which includes an hour a day for meals. Opportunities for promotion to Postal Executive C may occur after two years as a postal officer.

Engineering Apprenticeships

TRAINEE TECHNICIAN (APPRENTICE)

Open to young people aged 16 and 17, ideally having studied mathematical and scientific subjects to O level standard. This is a comprehensive three-year apprenticeship, covering all aspects of postal engineering, from lift systems, lighting, power, heating, ventilation to highly sophisticated automatic letter and parcel machinery. There are opportunities for concentrated training courses leading to the acquisition of recognised technical qualifications and practical on-the-job training is under the supervision of skilled engineers.

TRAINEE TECHNICIAN (IMPROVER)

Open to young people aged between 18 and 21. Full training is given for a limited range of duties and leads to being a qualified technician out in the field after a period of 12 months. Technical study is encouraged and after qualifying, further training is available for those who have proved their capabilities.

POSTAL EXECUTIVES B AND C

Applicants must be between the ages of 20 and 45. Selection is by interview and tests. Candidates should be graduates. Postal executives work in all areas of postal management, including operations,

marketing, personnel, finance, management services, buildings and
mechanisation. They are employed at Postal Headquarters in London
and in 10 regional offices throughout the country.

Further information

The Post Office Headquarters
33 Grosvenor Place
London SW1X 1PX
01-235 8000

The Post Office
Management Recruitment Centre
OMD 2-1 Management Assessment Centre
Coton House
Rugby
Warwickshire CV23 OBR
0788 74111

PRINTING

Printing is one of the top 10 UK manufacturing industries. Most print
works are 'closed shops', which means they only employ people who
belong to one of the print unions. The printing craftsman or technician
begins as an apprentice at 16 or 17 and then does a three- to four-year
training, depending on qualifications. Training schemes are run jointly
by the British Printing Industries Federation and the National Graphical
Association. Those with four O levels, including maths, a science and
English, can do a day-release or sandwich course for the BTEC award.

Further information

British Printing Industries Federation
11 Bedford Row
London WC1R 4DX
01-242 6904

Institute of Printing
8 Lonsdale Gardens
Tunbridge Wells
Kent TN1 1NU
0892 38118

Careers in Printing, Kogan Page

Where to look for jobs
Printing World
Lithoweek

PUBLIC RELATIONS

Although first-time entrants are increasingly of graduate standard
many people get into public relations via secretarial work; many also
start by working as an assistant in the public relations department of
a large company. A public relations officer is responsible for presenting
his company or client to the public in a favourable light, arranging for
interviews and articles to appear in the press and on TV and radio, and
for organising press parties and exhibitions. PR practitioners are
employed in consultancies, industrial and commercial firms, central
and local government, nationalised industries and a whole range of
voluntary bodies and non-profit organisations.
No qualifications are needed for entry at the secretarial level except
typing skills, and to progress you must have a pleasant, cheerful manner
and be able to talk easily to all sorts of people. If you decide to take
the part-time course leading to the CAM Diploma in Public Relations
you will need two A levels and three O levels including English language
to begin the CAM Foundation examinations.

Further information

Communications, Advertising and Marketing Foundation Ltd
Abford House
15 Wilton Road
London SW1V 1NJ
01-828 7506

The Institute of Public Relations
Gate House
St John's Square
London EC1M 4DH
01-253 5151

Careers in Marketing, Advertising and Public Relations, Kogan Page

Where to look for jobs

Campaign (weekly)
Daily Telegraph

RAILWAYS see British Rail

REMEDIAL GYMNAST see Physiotherapy

RESTAURANT WORK see Catering

RETAILING

Retailing is to do with the buying and selling of goods, and it is an industry that employs hundreds and thousands of people, from the floor cleaners in the big supermarkets up to the store managers. There are many different kinds of shops — local corner shops, selling newspapers and confectionery, chain stores, such as Woolworths or Marks and Spencer, department stores, such as Selfridges or Harrods, superstores and now even hypermarkets, which offer more or less everything under one roof. All shops, large or small, are involved in the business of selling goods to the public at a specified price.

It is easier to find a job in a large store, where there is a wider selection of jobs and better chances of promotion. Large companies are more likely to offer staff benefits, such as staff discounts, pension schemes, medical treatment, sports and social facilities, and perhaps most important, training schemes.

Whatever company you choose, and whatever level you enter, you will be expected to work long hours, and almost certainly on Saturdays, which is usually the busiest day for most shops (most companies give a day off in the week in return). You have to be fit, able to be on your feet for most of the day, and you have to have an interest in other people.

Manchester Polytechnic offers the first degree course in the UK, a BA (Hons) in Retail Marketing. It is a four-year sandwich course and includes two periods of of work experience. Students need five GCE subjects including two at A level; the O levels must include English language and maths; BTEC national certificate or diploma can be offered in lieu of A levels.

SALES STAFF

Personal qualities are more important that educational qualifications, though you should have a reasonable knowledge of arithmetic. You will need to look smart, be able to talk easily and clearly, and learn about the customers, the products sold and the methods of selling. Sales work provides essential training for higher level posts as supervisors, buyers, or managers.

Training

Entry qualifications vary from company to company. Some will only take on school-leavers with good CSE or O level grades, but others are more interested in people with personality, a willingness to work hard, and a reasonable standard in maths and English.

The Business and Technician Education Council and Scottish Vocational Education Council (BTEC/SCOTVEC) both offer a General Certificate for school-leavers aged 16-19 with few or no academic qualifications. It is suitable for junior trainees, sales assistants, supermarket employees, office clerks in distribution and employees in the the cooperative societies. There is also the BTEC and SCOTVEC National Certificate for school-leavers with four O levels or equivalent at A, B or C grade who have been taken on as sales assistants or office staff and have the potential to progress to positions such as trainee buyer, supervisor or manager of a small department.

CHECKOUT OPERATORS

Checkout operators work in supermarkets, freezer centres and self-service stores. Their job is to ring up customer purchases on a cash register. Some cash registers have devices for calculating the change, which is produced automatically.

In supermarkets, checkout operators are sometimes the only people the customer sees, and it is therefore very important that they are helpful and efficient. In quiet periods the operator will help out with other jobs such as shelf-filling. Operators will be expected to work on Saturdays, but will have a day off in lieu through the week. A new aspect to checkout work is laser scanning. Some large stores (such as the John Lewis Partnership) now have a computerised system. Each item is labelled with a magnetic code. The checkout operator passes purchases through a laser beam, the scanner picks up the code, converts it into electrical impulses which are transmitted to an in-store computer where price and product information is stored. The operator then presses a button for the total. The system can give an up-to-the-minute picture of sales of individual products, speeding up the process of stock-taking and re-ordering.

Training

Training is carried out in the supermarket or self-service store, usually by qualified instructors. They will be trained about security and what to do in cases of suspected shoplifting.

CASHIERS

Cashiers work in department stores, menswear shops, boutiques, TV and hi-fi stores etc. They operate cash registers and need to know about credit accounts and cheque acceptance/credit card procedures. They may also have to do some selling. As the job involves both handling money and dealing with customers, employers look for people who are responsible and trustworthy, neat, with a pleasant manner and a good standard of arithmetic.

Training

Training is carried out on the job and the larger shops and stores will also conduct off-the-job training sessions in subjects such as security and dealing with customers.

DISPLAY STAFF

Window displays, and displays inside the store, are essential to attract customers and encourage them to make a purchase. In a small store the manager will probably be in charge of display, but in large department stores and multiples there is usually a full-time display team headed by a display manager. The display team usually has its own workshop and storage areas and may make most of the 'props', using a wide range of materials. Some members of the team may spend all their time as studio artists, designing, making and painting the 'props'.

You need to have an interest in the merchandise, a good colour sense and manual dexterity. You also need to be fit and energetic, to carry around stepladders, mannequins, screens, piles of merchandise etc.

Training

School-leavers with three O levels or CSE Grade 1 can take a two-year full-time course leading to the BTEC Diploma, or find a job first and take a two-year part-time course. Some colleges, particularly the College for the Distributive Trades (address below) run their own courses.

RETAIL MANAGERS

The job of the manager varies considerably according to the size and type of the firm.

Branch Manager

The branch manager is responsible for the day-to-day running of the branch as laid down by head office. Most branch managers are responsible for recruiting and selecting staff and arranging for their training. They also control display and window dressing and have to monitor the general condition and maintenance of the premises. They are also responsible for stock levels, sales promotion and service to the customer. The daily cash balance has to be checked every night and the manager has to arrange for the cash to be taken to and from the bank. The branch manager may be responsible to head office direct, or to an area or regional manager.

Departmental Manager

The departmental manager is usually found in a department store. The post carries more responsibility than a branch manager. The departmental manager is responsible for buying and selling and will be in charge of a great number of staff. He will also be responsible for meeting sales targets, sales promotion, security and customer relations.

Supermarket Manager

The supermarket manager is head of a supermarket, superstore or hypermarket. You need to be fit, hard-working and practical, able to cope with pressure and think on your feet. You also have to be able to make decisions quickly. It requires foresight and planning, liaising with head office and considering the needs of the store weeks in advance. You have to keep an eye on all departments and know whether targets are being met or not. Managers are usually well educated, often up to degree standard.

Training

Most supermarket groups have trainee management schemes and recruit people with A levels or a business studies qualification, as well as graduates.

BUYERS

Buying requires wide knowledge in merchandising and selling. Shops turn round their stock several times a year, and if the wrong stock is bought money has been wasted. Overbuying will mean surplus stock, while underbuying will mean loss of customers, so the buyer has to get his/her sums right. The buyer has to decide what customers want, determine the range and level of stock, find suppliers, select merchandise, negotiate the best price and decide when and how much to buy.

In a small company there will only be one buyer, responsible for all these tasks; in larger firms there will be a team of buyers, each specialising in one area. Buyers are usually recruited from successful sales and management staff, so the first step if you are interested in becoming a buyer would be to join a firm as a member of the sales staff, or as a management trainee. There is opportunity to travel, both home and abroad, and some firms supply a company car.

Training

Most of the larger companies and department stores have their own training programmes. The Institute of Purchasing and Supply offers a Supervisory Course, for which the entry qualifications are four O levels, and a Professional Course for which you need five GCEs, two at A level. Many colleges offer full-time and part-time courses leading to these awards and there are also correspondence courses.

MERCHANDISER

The duties of the merchandiser vary from company to company. In some companies, the merchandiser will hold a senior position with responsibility for a range of merchandise, its content and price, and for giving guidelines to the buyers. In other firms, the merchandiser is in a more junior position, with responsibility for merchandise promotion, which includes display units, sales forecasts and stock levels.

Some companies specify O and A levels or a degree, while others ask for commonsense, an ability with figures and a willingness to work hard.

Training

The most suitable training courses are those offered by the Business and Technician Educational Council and the Scottish Vocational Education Council.

COMPUTER STAFF

The retailing industry is becoming increasingly computerised, and computer operators, programmers and systems analysts are in great demand. They are needed in three main areas: stock control and warehousing, where automated systems have been introduced; in stores which have article numbering or checkouts linked to computers; for applying information-processing systems to the administrative sector.

Training

Some of the larger companies have their own training programmes. Not all ask for O levels for trainee computer operators, though O and A levels are preferred. Sometimes operators progress to becoming programmers, but programmers are more likely to be recruited direct with A levels or a degree.

PERSONNEL MANAGER

The personnel manager recruits, trains and organises staff, administers
salaries and looks after health and welfare. The job will appeal to those
who like dealing with people. The personnel manager must be
approachable and able to act as counsellor when needed. He or she
must also be able to take the initiative and organise other people.
In a large firm, the personnel manager is head of a personnel
department. In smaller firms, he is under the store manager's
supervision.

Many people begin a career in personnel by starting on the sales side
or as a trainee staff manager. You will become an assistant personnel
manager after about six months. Depending on the company, you may
need A levels or a degree on entry.

Training

Many firms require their personnel staff to take the courses of the
Institute of Personnel Management or the National Examinations Board
for Supervisory Studies. Training in the store will last up to two years
and will normally consist of in-store and outside training schemes with
the emphasis on attaining staff management skills.

Further information

British Display Society
The Secretariat
Guardian House
92-94 Foxberry Road
London SE4 2SH
01-692 8943

Business and Technician Education Council (BTEC)
Central House
Upper Woburn Place
London WC1H 0HE
01-388 3288

College for the Distributive Trades
30 Leicester Square
London WC2H 7LE
01-839 1547

Cooperative College
Stanford Hall
Loughborough
Leicestershire LE12 5QR
050-982 2333

Institute of Personnel Management
IPM House
35 Camp Road
London SW19 4UW
01-946 9100

Institute of Purchasing and Supply
Easton House
Easton-on-the-Hill
Stamford
Lincolnshire PE9 3NZ
0780 56670

Manchester Polytechnic
All Saints
Manchester M15 6BH

National Examinations Board for Supervisory Studies
76 Portland Place
London W1N 4AA
01-580 3050

Scottish Vocational Education Council
22 Great King Street
Edinburgh EH3 6QH
031-557 4555

Careers in Retailing, Kogan Page

ROYAL AIR FORCE see The Armed Forces
ROYAL NAVY see The Armed Forces

SECRETARIAL WORK

Secretarial work can cover a wide range of activities, from copy-typing to being someone's personal secretary. The job you get depends very much not only on your shorthand and typing skills, but also on your poise, general level of education and willingness to accept responsibility.

The copy-typist types simple correspondence, memos and invoices. The job has been made easier by electric typewriters and photocopying machines, but she still has to do a lot of routine chores. The shorthand-typist must be able to write shorthand at 90 - 100 wpm and must have a reasonable command of English, including being able to spell. She must be able to produce well-written and typed letters from her shorthand notes. The audio-typist works directly from a dictating machine.

The personal secretary is not only an excellent typist, but she also looks after the office and does much of the employer's routine work. A sense of initiative is vital, together with tact and good sense, as you will be answering the phone and dealing with day-to-day problems in the office.

Training
There is a wide range of courses available, leading to the Certificates and Diplomas of the Royal Society of Arts, the London Chamber of Commerce, Pitman, as well as the BTEC and SCOTVEC awards.

If you have done a commercial course at school you can probably find a job as a clerk or typist. Those with fewer than four O levels can do one- to two-year courses leading to jobs as clerks and shorthand-typists. There are also one- to two-year courses for those with up to five O levels, teaching secretarial skills. For the BTEC awards, you can study while on the job, through day-release or block-release. With less than four O levels you begin with a General award.

See also Medical Secretary; Office Work

Further information

Business and Technician Education Council
Central House
Upper Woburn Place
London WC1H 0HH
01-388 3288

London Chamber of Commerce and Industry
Commercial Education Scheme
Marlowe House
Station Road
Sidcup
Kent DA15 7BJ
01-302 0261

Pitman Examinations Institute
Catteshall Manor
Godalming, Surrey GU7 1UU
04868 5311

Royal Society of Arts Examinations Board
John Adam Street
Adelphi
London WC2N 6EZ
01-839 2366

Scottish Vocational Educational Council
22 Great King Street
Edinburgh EH3 6QH
031-557 4555

Contact your Local Education Authority (find number in the phone book) for a list of colleges offering relevant courses.

Where to find jobs

Daily Telegraph
Guardian
Free magazines (in London) such as *Ms London*
Local press, particularly evening papers

SELLING & MARKETING

The marketing and sales staff in any business or organisation are the people who persuade the public, via shops and stores, to buy the goods produced by their firm. The product they are selling can be anything from books to baked beans, but in each case they have to find out what the customer wants and arrange for it to get into the shops, perhaps organising an advertising campaign at the same time to create a 'demand' for it. The most usual way to start is as a sales representative (the 'rep'). He or she travels around the country persuading shops and stores to stock the product, arranging window displays, handing out specially designed display material and organising special promotions, all with the aim of selling more of the product.

No special entry qualifications are required, except perhaps a driving licence, but you need to be self-confident, finding it easy to chat to people of all kinds. You also need to be quick-witted and good at grasping figures easily. Selling is not a job for sensitive plants, as you will have to put up with a lot of rebuffs and even rudeness. You will also have to be willing to be away from home a lot.

See also Retailing.

Further information

Institute of Marketing
Moor Hall
Cookham
Maidenhead
Berkshire SL6 9QH
06285 24922

Careers in Marketing, Advertising and Public Relations, Kogan Page

Where to find jobs

Daily Telegraph
Local press, particularly evening papers

SOCIAL WORK

Social work is done in social services departments in local government, the probation and aftercare service, in hospitals, residential homes for the young and old, and in education. To become a *professional* social worker you need the Certificate of Qualification in Social Work: there are various approaches depending on your academic qualifications and at what stage you decide to go in for social work. If you are over 20 and have five O levels, you can take a two-year full-time course at a college or polytechnic. If you are under 20, you need two A levels to do a three- to four-year degree course.

If you want to do social work but lack the academic qualifications you can work in one of the residential homes for children or old people, or for the physically or mentally handicapped. The work is demanding and the hours tend to be long, but it is good training, particularly if you hope one day to become properly qualified. (It is worth remembering that in general, the older and more mature you are the less formal GCE-type qualifications matter. Over-25s can be accepted on courses for the CQSW without normal GCEs, particularly if you already have some practical experience.)

If you take a job as a home help organiser, a social work assistant, or become a member of staff in a residential home or in a special school, you can take a Certificate in Social Service (CSS). For this, you must be 18 and have five GCEs (A, B or C) if you are under 21.

YOUTH AND COMMUNITY WORKERS

Workers are usually attached to a community centre which will include not only a youth club but also toddler clubs, adventure playgrounds, painting classes, classes for immigrants, etc. Community workers can be employed by social services departments, by education departments with youth clubs or community centres. Voluntary organisations working with youth, inter-racial groups and welfare rights groups also use community workers. Workers take a two-year full-time diploma or certificate course, for which you need five O levels for entry. There are also Regional Community Work Training Groups who organise training courses in local areas. See address below.

Further information

Your local council

British Association of Social Workers
16 Kent Street
Birmingham B5 6RD
021-622 3911

Federation of Community Work Training Corps
10 Wharncliffe Road
Sheffield S10 2DH

Central Council for Education and Training in Social Work
Derbyshire House
St Chad's Street
London WC1H 8AD
01-278 2455

Ivanhoe House
9 South St David Street
Edinburgh EH2 2BW
031-556 2953

West Wing
St David's House
Wood Street,
Cardiff CF1 1ES
0222 26257

Careers in Social Work, Kogan Page
Jobs in Community Care, Kogan Page

Where to look for jobs

Community Care
Guardian
Opportunities (weekly)
Local press
Municipal Journal

SPEECH THERAPY

This is an increasingly important medical area. Applicants should be
18 and have at least five O levels including English language, and two
A levels. Graduates may apply for a special two-year course. Otherwise,
the main route to qualification is a three-year diploma course at a
recognised school. Competition for places is considerable and the
diploma course is tough, containing a good deal of theory which makes
a science background desirable.

Further information

The College of Speech Therapists
Harold Poster House
6 Lechmere Road
London NW2 5BU
01-459 8521

SURVEYOR see Estate Agent

TELECOMMUNICATIONS see British Telecom

TRAFFIC WARDEN

The job of the traffic warden is sometimes thankless; a sense of humour and the ability to stay calm and unruffled are obviously important. Most of your day will be concerned with parking offences, but you might also be called upon to do school crossing patrol or traffic control duty, which call for considerable skill and self confidence.

You need to be fit and healthy, as this is an outdoors job, and with good eyesight. The age limit is 18-59.

Training

Traffic wardens come under the control of the police (in London the Metropolitan Police). There is a three-week training course before you begin. Training is given by police and traffic warden instructors. It includes: traffic laws and regulations, hand signals when controlling traffic, giving evidence in court, emergency first aid at accidents, how to deal with irate motorists.

There is a five-rung ladder of promotion, leading from traffic warden, traffic warden supervisor, traffic warden controller, senior traffic warden controller up to divisional traffic warden controller.

Further information

Metropolitan Police Office
Dept E8, Room 214
105 Regency Street
London SW1P 4AN
01-230 3717

Outside London apply to your nearest Regional Police Headquarters — you will find the address and telephone number in your local telephone directory.

TRAVEL & TOURISM

In a travel office you start as a clerk, learning to do the paperwork involved in arranging and booking tours, and you can then be promoted to counter selling, advising and arranging tours and holidays. Senior operators go abroad to try out different holidays and facilities. The job demands a high degree of accuracy. Most people train on the job while taking evening classes or a correspondence course for the examinations of the Institute of Travel and Tourism. Minimum qualifications are four O levels and knowledge of a language is obviously an advantage.

Further information

Association of British Travel Agents
11-17 Chertsey Road
Woking
Surrey GU21 5AL
04862 27321

The Institute of Travel and Tourism
113 Victoria Street
St Albans
Hertfordshire AL1 3JT
0727 54395

Careers in the Holiday Industry, Kogan Page
Jobs in Travel and Tourism, Kogan Page

Where to look for jobs

Travelnews (weekly)
Travel Trade Gazette (weekly)
Local press, particularly evening papers

TYPING see Computers, Office Work, Secretarial Work

VETERINARY NURSE

The veterinary nurse assists the veterinary surgeon in the surgery. The work involves holding animals during treatment, looking after instruments, preparing medicines and assisting during operations. You obviously need to be an animal-lover and it helps if you are not squeamish.

Training, which lasts at least years, is done on the job with day-release, block-release or evening courses. To enrol you must be employed at a veterinary practice or hospital approved by the Royal College of Veterinary Surgeons, you must be 17 and have four O levels, CSE grade 1 or SCE O grade passes including English language and a science subject or maths.

Further information

The Royal College of Veterinary Surgeons
32 Belgrave Square
London SW1X 8QP
01-235 4971

Careers in Veterinary Surgery, Kogan Page
Careers Working with Animals, Kogan Page

VETERINARY WORK see Animal Technician, Veterinary Nurse

WAITER/WAITRESS see Catering

WORD PROCESSING see Computers, Office Work

YOUTH WORK see Social Work

Chapter 3

IMPROVING YOUR CHANCES

FURTHER EDUCATION AND TRAINING

Whether you left school without bothering to sit any exams and now find that you are not qualified for the jobs you would like; or you have found a job but need to learn the special skills that go with it if you are going to progress at all, the answer is in further education and training.

There are some 600 colleges of further education all over the country offering a wide range of courses. You can study for the O levels or A levels needed for the job you want; you can study for the various levels of professional exams (eg banking) working yourself up the promotion ladder through day-release or evening study; or you can take a vocational course, ie geared to a particular kind of work, such as mechanical engineering, audio-typing, gas-fitting etc.

Many of these colleges offer the Business and Technician Education Council awards which have gradually replaced the old National Certificates and Diplomas. The advantage of these new awards is their flexibility: you work for units or modules — aspects of a subject — which then add up to a Certificate or Diploma. Also, you are not tied down to full-time or part-time. You can start with a full-time course and then go on to part-time when you have found a job. Study, in fact, can be how you want: full-time, day-release, block-release or evening. There are no rigid entry qualifications — you slot in at whatever level you are suited for. All that is required for the most basic level is that you must be 16 and have completed a normal secondary school education course or equivalent.

BTEC/SCOTVEC courses

BTEC courses offer nationally recognised qualifications (other than degrees) in a wide range of subjects in the following main occupational fields: agriculture; business and finance; computing and information systems; construction; design; distributive, hotel and catering and leisure services; engineering; public administration and science. There are also more general pre-vocational courses and a range of continuing education studies.

Courses leading to BTEC awards are run in colleges and polytechnics and, in some cases, schools throughout England, Wales and Northern Ireland. They can be studied through different modes including full-time, day-release and evening, block-release, sandwich and, where appropriate, correspondence courses and other 'open learning' arrangements. The detailed content of courses may vary from centre to centre to reflect local and regional needs.

If you want to know about a particular course in your area, your local college, careers office or education authority will be able to help. For other information please write to The BTEC Information Office, Central House, Upper Woburn Place, London WC1H 0HH.

For information about courses in Scotland contact Scottish Vocational Education Council (SCOTVEC), 22 Great King Street, Edinburgh EH3 6QH; 031-557 4555.

City and Guilds Certificates

Through its examinations and certificates City and Guilds provides recognised national standards in a wide range of technical and craft subjects. The courses and examinations are designed for a wide variety of jobs in the following broad industrial groups:

Agriculture, Horticulture and Forestry — Mining and Quarrying — Chemical, Metallurgical and Allied Industries — Food and Drink — Engineering — Personal Services and Community Care — Vehicles — Textiles — Clothing, Footwear and Leather — Travel, Tourism and Recreation — Printing and Paper — Furniture — Construction — Gas, Electricity and

Water — Hotels and Catering — Professional, Scientific and
Miscellaneous Services — Creative Studies.

Courses are run in technical colleges, colleges of further
education and other educational establishments and schools.
Most courses start in September, but there are many
that start at other times of the year. Courses are part-time
(attendance for one day and often one evening a week)
or full-time (attendance on each day during the week);
the full length of each course varies considerably, from as
little as one term to as much as three years.

For more information ask your careers teacher, the careers
service, or your employer. Or write to the City and Guilds of
London Institute, 76 Portland Place, London W1N 4AA.

Commercial, secretarial and language courses

The Royal Society of Arts and the London Chamber of
Commerce are the two main bodies that offer commercial,
secretarial and language qualifications. Many colleges all over
the country run full-time and part-time courses leading to
their examinations. For details of courses, either contact
your local college or write to The Royal Society of Arts
Examinations Board, 6-8 John Adam Street, Adelphi,
London WC2N 6EZ, telephone 01-839 1691, or The London
Chamber of Commerce and Industry, Commercial Education
Scheme, Marlowe House, Station Road, Sidcup, Kent
DA15 7BJ, telephone 01-302 0261.

Regional Examining Bodies

In England and Wales these bodies offer a wide range of
courses in vocational subjects at various levels. These courses
can be full-time, part-time, sandwich or evening, and cover
their own awards as well as BTEC awards, RSA and London
Chamber of Commerce awards and the Certificates and
Diplomas of various professional bodies such as the Institute
of Bankers. Each body can give you information on college
courses over a wide area. For details of courses available
contact:

London and Home Counties
Regional Advisory Council for
Technological Education
Tavistock House South
Tavistock Square
London WC1H 9LR

East Anglia
Regional Advisory Council for
Further Education
Shire Hall
Bury St Edmunds
Suffolk IP33 2AN

North West
Regional Advisory Council for
Further Education
The Town Hall
Walkden Road
Worsley
Manchester M28 4QE

South
Regional Council for
Further Education
26 Bath Road
Reading RG1 6NT

South West
Regional Council for
Further Education
2nd Floor
37-38 Fore Street
Taunton
Somerset TA1 1HR

East Midlands
Regional Advisory Council for the
Organisation of Further Education
Robins Wood House
Robins Wood Road
Aspley, Nottingham NG8 3NH

North
Advisory Council for
Further Education
5 Grosvenor Villas
Grosvenor Road
Newcastle-upon-Tyne NE2 2RU

West Midlands
Advisory Council for
Further Education
Norfolk House
Smallbrook Queensway
Birmingham B5 4NB

Yorkshire and Humberside
Council for Further Education
Bowling Green Terrace
Jack Lane
Leeds LS11 9SX

Wales
Welsh Joint Education
Committee
245 Western Avenue
Cardiff CF5 2YX

Apprenticeships

In some industries (eg the building industry or the various branches of engineering) the traditional way in is through an apprenticeship. The employer takes you on (usually at 16 to 17) and gives you a training for three to four years while you work for him. Nowadays this training also involves day- or block-release classes at college while you study for the relevant City and Guilds Certificates, or for the BTEC awards.

The apprenticeship is a formal contract between you and the employer and it usually has to be witnessed by your parents or guardian. It is a very good way of training. You are paid (though not very highly) while you are an apprentice and you are more or less guaranteed employment once you have successfully completed your apprenticeship.

HOW TO FIND OUT ABOUT APPRENTICESHIPS

Unfortunately, there is no central body that administers apprenticeships. Within each industry, it is the individual employer who decides whether or not he takes on apprentices and what standard of education he will want. Generally, you will be required to have four GCEs/CSEs. Ask your careers officer or Jobcentre for the names of local firms that take on apprentices or write to:

Building Industry Careers Service
82 New Cavendish Street
London W1M 8AD

Construction Industry
Training Board
Bircham Newton
King's Lynn
Norfolk PE31 6RH
048 523 291 (ext 213)

The Engineering Careers
Information Service
54 Clarendon Road
Watford WD1 1LB
0923 38441

Road Transport Industry
Training Board
Capitol House, Empire Way,
Wembley
Middlesex HA9 0NG
01-902 8880
and Regional Offices

The Ministry of Defence takes on a large number of apprentices every year. For details of apprenticeships offered by the Army, Navy, RAF and WRAF see *The Armed Forces*, (p 25) or ask your local Careers Service.

Chapter 4

STARTING THE SEARCH

Where to start

Now that you know *what kind* of job you are looking for and whether you have the necessary qualifications, you can begin the job-hunt in earnest. Remember that the more jobs you apply for, the more likelihood there is of your finding one. You will be giving yourself not only a better chance, but a better choice. Sometimes the problem is not that there are no jobs, but that the right person has not applied for the right vacancy. You are also wasting time and opportunities if you only apply for one job at a time. Apply for all the jobs you can find (provided you are not wildly unsuitable for them).

Remember too that refusals happen to everyone, so don't get discouraged.

Where to look

NEWSPAPERS

National daily papers such as *The Times*, the *Daily Telegraph* and the *Guardian* carry a lot of advertisements for jobs. Don't be put off if there is nothing the first time you look — get into the habit of looking at the papers *every day* just on the off-chance. There is no need to go to the expense of buying papers. If you can't borrow them from someone who takes a paper regularly, the reading-room of your local library will have them.

Local papers are an even better bet for finding jobs. A big evening paper such as the *London Standard* advertises hundreds of jobs of all kinds. In London, *magazines* such as

Time Out carry many job advertisements. You should also look at the *free newspapers and magazines* given away (at tube stations or pushed through your letter box) as they are also a good source of jobs. Wherever you live, there will be a morning or evening paper (sometimes both) that covers your area, and often there is a weekly paper as well.

Jobs in daily papers tend to be snapped up quickly and are not likely to be re-advertised, so make sure you apply *at once* if you see something. Next week will be too late. Remember too that 'evening' papers are often on the news-stands by early afternoon, and the *London Standard* is on sale at 10 am. at 10 am.

SPECIALIST MAGAZINES AND NEWSPAPERS

A lot of trades and professions have their own paper or magazine where jobs are advertised — nurses can look in *Nursing Times and Nursing Mirror*, for example. These papers will give you a very good idea of what sort of jobs are going and might even give you more ideas about jobs you could apply for. Most big newsagents (the ones on railway stations, for instance) stock these specialist papers and again, if you don't want to buy them, you can see them in the reading-room of your local library.

Remember to make sure that is the *current* issue you look at! The weeklies usually come out on a particular day. If you are specially interested in one, find out what day it comes out and make sure you are there early to look at it — you will probably find that the best jobs are all taken that same day, so it pays to get there first.

Reading specialist papers will also have the benefit of giving you more idea of what to expect of a job in that field.

JOBCENTRES

Most towns have a Jobcentre (London has around 50). There is no need to feel nervous of going into one — you can wander in, browse round the shelves and wander out again without speaking to anyone, if you want. They are designed like supermarkets, with the jobs displayed on boards up and down the room. Each job has a card giving you the details. If you like the sound of it, you can take the card up to the desk and the staff will arrange an interview for you. If you want to chat and ask for advice, the staff can give you lots of information on suitable jobs, which firms to approach about apprenticeships, what training schemes are available. They can also put you in touch with Jobcentres in other areas, if you don't want to work locally. The Jobcentre is usually in your local high street, but if you don't know where to find it, look in the local telephone directory.

EMPLOYMENT AGENCIES

These are commercially owned agencies advertising jobs. The employer pays the agency to find them the right people to fill their jobs. You don't have to pay anything. The agencies often specialise in particular kinds of work, such as catering, nursing or secretarial jobs. But some have a complete range of skilled and unskilled jobs at all levels. Look in the Yellow Pages for your area under 'Employment Agencies'. Like the Jobcentre, you can go in and browse until you find something suitable, only in this case the agency is in the role of employer and therefore you should make an effort as you would for an interview (see Chapter 6).

SOME SPECIALIST EMPLOYMENT AGENCIES

BUILDING TRADES

Montrose Technical Staff Ltd
1 Wilton Road
London SW1 1LL
01-834 3406

They place people all over the country — contact the London office.

P J Mulvaney & Co Ltd
155 Kingston Road
London SW19 1LJ
01-542 0091
01-543 3111

Their area covers southern England and the Home Counties.

CLERKS, BOOKKEEPERS ETC

Accountancy Appointments
Wren House
4 Bear Street
London WC2H 7AR
01-434 1632

Accountancy Engagements
78 Queen Victoria Street
London EC4N 4SJ
01-248 6071, 236 0691

Accountancy Personnel Assignments Ltd
63-65 Moorgate
London EC2R 6BH
01-628 9015

Branches in: Barking 01-594 7613
Birmingham 021-643 6201
Cardiff 0222 371 446
Croydon 01-686 4686
Leeds 0532 438384
Leicester 0533 542693
Manchester 061-834 9733
Nottingham 0742 582939
Wolverhampton 0902 771975

Accountancy Recruitment
262 Regent Street
London W1R 5DA
01-734 3892

Accounting Appointments
7 Princes Street
London W1R 7RB
01-629 7262

Acme Agency
315 Oxford Street
London W1R 1LA
01-493 4000

Bookkeepers Bureau
118 New Bond Street
London W1Y 9AB
01-493 9441

COMPUTER PERSONNEL/ENGINEERS/DRAUGHTSMEN

Compass Technical Services
181 Chiswick High Road
London W4 2DR
01-995 4546

DOMESTIC STAFF/COOKS/HOUSEKEEPERS

Belgravia Bureau
35 Brompton Road
London SW3 1DE
01-225 0327

Domesticare Employment Agency
1c Lithos Road
London NW3 6DX
01-794 1466

Jubilee Catering Agency
25 Frith Street
London W1V 5TR
01-437 5074

ENGINEERING/DRAUGHTSMEN/ELECTRICIANS

Leppel Engineering Services Ltd
25 Victoria Street
London SW1H 0EX
01-222 0656

Montrose Technical Staff Ltd
1 Wilton Road
London SW1V 1LL
01-834 3406

They place staff all over the country — contact the London office.

NURSERY NURSES

Brompton Bureau
10 Beauchamp Place
London SW3 1NQ
01-584 6242

NURSING

British Nursing Association
443 Oxford Street
London W1R 2NA
01-629 9030

London Nurses Agency Ltd
68 Great Portland Street
London W1N 5AL
01-580 0105

Marylebone Nursing Service
2 Darnley Terrace
London W11 4RL
01-603 3746

PUBLIC RELATIONS

J F Consultants
9 Blenheim Street
New Bond Street
London W1Y 9LE
01-493 6212

SCIENTIFIC STAFF

Scientific Staff Consultants
50 Lincoln's Inn Fields
London WC2A 3PF
01-831 6471

SECRETARIES, OFFICE STAFF

Alfred Marks Bureau Ltd
84 Regent Street
London W1R 5PA
01-437 7855

Belgravia Bureau
35 Brompton Road
London SW3 1DE
01-225 0327

Brook Street Bureau
63 Oxford Street
London W1R 1RB
01-437 7711

Kelly Girl
87-91 New Bond Street
London W1Y 9LA
01-409 0027

Reed Employment
181-183 Victoria Street
London SW1E 5NE
01-828 5168

Branches in all large towns — look in your local telephone
directory for the nearest, or contact the London branch for
information.

Drake Personnel
Head Office:
225 Regent Street
London W1R 7DB
01-734 0911

Stella Fisher Bureau
110 Strand
London WC2R 0AA
01-836 6644

Who can help you?

Make sure that all friends, acquaintances and friends of
friends know that you are job-hunting, especially those
who are working. Someone might know of a vacancy
coming up at work, or might have spotted an ad that you
have overlooked. It is always a help to have other people
looking out for you. This way, you might even get to hear
about a job before it is advertised.

Don't be shy of asking for help from your public library. If
you have never even set foot in the library before, now is the
time to start. The reference section will have daily papers
as well as specialist magazines, and if the staff don't have
anything they will probably be able to tell you where to

get it. The reference section will also have telephone directories, addresses of Jobcentres and directories which list firms according to their type of business. Remember that the library is a public service which you (or your parents) pay for through the rates — so make use of it. The reference librarian is *not* an ogre but someone who has been trained to help people look for things — make use of him or her.

Don't spurn the help of your school or college careers service. Once you know what sort of job you are looking for, they will be in a much better position to help you. They will know which firms to approach and where to apply for training schemes or apprenticeships.

Firms you would like to work for

Instead of waiting for ads to come up, you can try writing directly to employers and firms. Look in the Yellow Pages of the telephone directory where companies are listed by types of business, eg gardening, taxis etc or ask in the reference section of your local public library: they will have directories listing firms according to their activities (engineering, publishing, decorating etc). You can then write a letter on the off-chance they might have a vacancy or might be willing to take on a trainee. (See p 138 for an example of a letter written 'on spec'.) it is well worthwhile writing on the off-chance like this, particularly if you are very keen on a certain job. Employers like people who sound enthusiastic and might decide to see you anyhow, even if they hadn't been planning to take on anyone new. And who knows, your letter might arrive the day someone decides to hand in their notice!

Be organised

You may be a working-with-your-hands type who finds paperwork difficult, but we can assure you that it is well worthwhile getting yourself organised when you are looking for a job. Ask a tidy-minded friend or relative to help you if you really feel this is all beyond you.

First — get yourself a file. A ring binder or cardboard envelope file and some cardboard dividers will hold everything to do with your job-hunting. *If you're organised from the start it's much easier and will help in your search.* It's very easy to think that you can remember what you've written or who you've applied to when you begin, but if you take the search seriously it won't be long before you wish you had · kept a copy of one of your letters or written down a telephone number or some other essential information in a safe place.

A file containing the following helps a lot:

1. List of personal details and aims
2. Letters
3. Plans for action
4. Certificates, Diplomas etc you have won.

1. PERSONAL DETAILS AND AIMS

If you do a neat and readable list of your personal details and aims you can refer to it each time you apply for a job whether by telephone, letter or application form. It will be particularly useful if you have to speak on the telephone because it is easy to become tongue-tied, empty-headed or muddled. You can use it as a checklist when you write a letter too, just to see if there's any essential information you've left out. It's often the most obvious facts which are left out. You won't always need all the items on the list at the same time, but if they are all in one place you can use them all or select as you need.

Include:
- ☐ Education — names and addresses of schools, college, training courses, and the dates you attended them.
- ☐ Qualifications obtained.
- ☐ Interests, hobbies, spare-time jobs and activities.
- ☐ Referees — names, addresses and telephone numbers.

Keep any notes you made in assessing yourself on a separate sheet in this part of the file.

If you need a curriculum vitae (essential details of your life to date) keep copies of it in this section too. See p 142. You should also keep a list of all applications you make.

2. LETTERS

Do a carbon copy of every letter you write or take a xerox
(there are copying machines in most large libraries and main
railway stations). Then you always know what you've said
if you are called to interview and you also have a format you
can alter and improve upon as you think suitable each time
you apply for another job. When the reply comes clip it to
your copy of your letter. Keep all the correspondence with
a firm including any copies of application forms, the original
advertisement and any leaflets or information you have
about them together, so that you have the whole picture in
one place.

You could keep your batches of information and
correspondence with each firm either in groups of similar
types of jobs or simply in alphabetical order by the name
of the firm.

Keep notes about telephone calls here as well.

3. PLANS FOR ACTION

This is where to put all your notes and scraps of paper about
things to do. Write down any ideas you have or suggestions
from other people. See the section 'Where to start' earlier in
this chapter to help you begin.

Think of people whose advice you could ask on careers in
general and specific jobs and where to find them, eg friends/
acquaintances with jobs you like the sound of, teachers,
careers officers, people you've done holidays jobs for.

Think of companies you are interested in.

Make a note of and act on any scraps of information you can
find about where to look for jobs advertised or information
about jobs. Each day you can look to see if there's anything
you can do. Buy a magazine? Ring a friend? Write to an
organisation?

4. CERTIFICATES AND DIPLOMAS

It's important to keep these in a safe place, so you can be
sure of finding them when needed.

131

DATE APPLIED	NAME OF JOB	EMPLOYER	WHERE HEARD ABOUT	HOW APPLIED	REPLY	NEXT
14.5.86	—	Wobbobley Ltd	On off chance	Letter	No vacancies	—
15.5.86	Apprentice	A. Wokes Ltd	'Evening Argus' 15.5.86	Phone	Interview 19.5.86	
15.5.86	Apprentice Fitter	Taylor Munray & Co Ltd	Job Centre	Letter		
15.5.86	Several vacancies	Plum Agricultural Machinery	Bob's friend	Phone	They've sending form	Fill in form
15.5.86	Engineering course	Halford Technical College	'Guide to Careers'	Letter	Prospectus	
16.5.86	Apprentice	Croxley Consultant Engineers	'Engineering Today' (May)	Phone	Post filled	—
16.5.86	Apprentice	Benn & Howarth	'The Herald' 16th May	Phone		Write with details
16.5.86	—	Harricks Ltd	On off chance	Letter	Vacancy list	Phone call – interview 19.5.86

A day-to-day check list of your applications helps you keep track

Chapter 5

APPLICATIONS

The employer usually specifies the way in which he wishes
you to apply. If not specified, it is quicker to answer by
telephone. Read the description of the job and the
instructions it gives for application very carefully and do
what it says. Normally it will ask you to apply in writing or
by telephone giving details or requesting an application form.
The aim of your application is to get an interview. This is the
first impression that the employer has of you and you don't
want it to be the last. Below we give examples of the basic
rules and common sense needed at this point.

Writing letters

Appearance

Any letter you write, no matter who it is addressed to,
should look tidy and use clear English. Casual notes or
scribbles or unreadable messes will just lose you the job.

Remember that the appearance of your letter will help the
employer to decide whether or not to offer you an interview.
It's really worth taking trouble.

Contents

The best rule is to keep your letter short and to the point
unless you have been asked for a detailed description of your
qualifications and background. You will be given an
opportunity to give full details at a later stage if your first
letter is successful. Be accurate and truthful and remember
that when it comes to the interview the employer is likely to
question you on whatever you have written or said earlier.

The date ————————————————————————————

Name of person to whom you are writing ————————
if you know it and/or position.
It's always better if you can find a name

Name and address of firm ————————————————

Reference number if one is given ——————————

Name or Sir (or Madam) if name unknown ——————

Job title ———————————————————————
Where you saw it advertised ——————————————
Why you are interested*

Whether you have any experience or not ——————————
and whether you have anything in particular to offer*

If appropriate, mention qualifications ——————————
or that you enclose list
of them/curriculum vitae

When you are available for interview ————————————

'Yours faithfully' is correct unless ————————
you know the person's name — then
put 'Yours sincerely'.

Print your name clearly beneath ————————
your signature (& title if female)

*Try to be honest and positive. Think of
what **they are looking for.**

```
                                        15 Essex Road,
                                        Harpenden,
                                        Herts AL5 4HQ

                                        7 March 1986

Personnel Manager,
Harold Smith & Co Ltd,
Smith House,
Station Road,
Harpenden,
Herts.

..........

Dear Sir,

I should like to apply for the appointment (job/
position/vacancy) of ............... advertised
in the ............. of/on ............. (date).
This job is of particular interest to me because
............... and, while I have as yet no
experience, I think ............... .


I enclose a list of my qualifications/details of
my education and work experience to date.  I
shall be pleased to provide any further details
required.  I am free to come for interview at
any time.

Yours faithfully,

John Smith

John Smith
```

Sample letter applying for advertised vacancy

PLEASE REMEMBER: IF YOU ARE MORE OR LESS REPEATING A
STANDARD LETTER, FROM THIS BOOK OR ANYWHERE ELSE,
BE CERTAIN THAT YOU HAVE CHANGED ALL THE NECESSARY
INFORMATION, TO FIT YOUR SITUATION!

135

(Your address)

(Date)

(Firm's name and address)

(Reference number, if one is
given in the advertisement)

Dear Sir,

Please will you send me particulars of the position
advertised in .... on .... (date)
together with an application form (if the
advertisement mentions one).

Yours faithfully,

(Your signature)

(Your name printed clearly
underneath signature)

Sample letter asking for details of an advertised job

```
                                        (Your address)

                                        (Date)


     (Firm's name and address)

     (Reference number, if one is
     given in the advertisement)


     Dear Sir, (or name if you have had a letter giving
     you a name)

     Thank you for your letter of .......... (date).
     I enclose my completed application form.

     I look forward to hearing from you. I am free to
     come for interview at any time convenient to you
     but should appreciate as much notice as possible.

     I am ......... (what you can offer/why you are
     applying or simply that you are prepared to work
     hard).

     Yours faithfully, (or Yours sincerely if you have
     written to a named person)




     (Your signature)

     (Your name printed clearly
     underneath signature)
```

Sample letter accompanying an application form

(Your address)

(Date)

(Firm's name and address)

Dear Sir,

I am looking for an opening in ....
(type of work) and am writing to ask if
.... (firm's name) has any vacancies
which might be suitable.

I enclose details of my education and particular
interests. I am particularly keen to become a
.... (type of job) because ....
..... .

I realise that you may not have any vacancies.
I should be grateful, however, for any advice you
can give and hope that I may come and see you or
one of your staff.

I look forward to hearing from you.

Yours faithfully,

Sample on-spec letter
to a firm which has not advertised a vacancy
but where you hope there might be a suitable opening for you.

*(Address to the Managing Director or, in the case of a very large firm,
to the Personnel Officer. Wherever possible take the trouble to find
out their name (eg by ringing the switchboard).*

Rough copy

Whether you are writing on-spec letters or replying to an advertised vacancy it's a good idea to do a rough copy first. Make it a neat rough and you'll be able to see how long it is, how it looks and how it sounds. Make sure that nothing is left out or spelt incorrectly and make any necessary alterations. Don't write your life history — try to make it concise. It should contain enough information to make it possible for the employer to consider you as a likely candidate and to offer you an interview where further information can be exchanged. See the examples on the preceding pages.

The final copy should be well spaced and clearly written. Good typing is acceptable and may even help your application for certain jobs where it will be a necessary skill. Use ink, not pencil, and proper plain writing paper. Set it out correctly as in the examples given. (It is safest to use plain writing paper because some people do not approve of coloured, lined or patterned paper.)

There are many different ways of writing these letters which would be acceptable. Examples are given on pages 134-8 to help you.

ON-SPEC LETTERS

Write to firms in the area you are interested in. Inquire whether they have any vacancies and/or ask if they could help you to learn more about the type of work they do or give you some general advice. They might be able to send you a brochure, or show you around, or invite you to talk to the personnel officer or manager, or recommend a training course, and so on. The clearer you are about what the job entails, the easier it will be to know if it is right for you and the better you will do in interviews.

Write to the Personnel Officer or Appointments Officer in large firms and to the Managing Director or Manager in smaller companies. Ring up the receptionist and find out the correct name to write to — it will help to get your letter to the right person.

You could also say that you realise they may not have an immediate vacancy but would like to be informed when a vacancy for which you are suitable does arise.

Applying by telephone

Quite often advertisements ask you to ring a number. Before you pick up the phone have your list of personal details with you, a copy of the advertisement, and write yourself a note about why you are applying for the job.

When you ring, speak clearly, be polite, and explain which job you are applying for and where you heard of it. They may take some initial details to check that you are a possible candidate and then ask for your address in order to send you an application form. Or they might find out enough to invite you for interview Try as far as possible to be available when they invite you to come. If you can't go at the times they suggest, say why. It won't help very much if you say that you're going to the sales that day — make it a good reason.

Inviting you to apply by telephone is a way of sorting out applicants at an early stage. Be prepared and treat it as if it counts.

Filling in application forms

Even if you have already given your particulars in a letter or a curriculum vitae you should still complete an application form if you are sent one because it will fit in with the system the firm uses and be easier for them.

— Write neatly and clearly.

— Follow the instructions.

— Answer the questions precisely.

— As you become used to filling in forms it will be easier but you should read each new form carefully. Read it right through at the start.

— Fill it in in pencil first to make sure it fits and to think about your answers. Check it and then fill it in in ink and in block capitals, or however it instructs. Your list of personal details will help you here. Common mistakes are to muddle the information, eg Nationality: Church of England; or to misinterpret the information required, eg Place of Birth: 'at home' (instead of Manchester, London etc).

— Read the advertisement or company literature again before answering the sort of question that asks you why you want the job and what reasons make you think you would be suitable. If you are planning some kind of further training in this field, eg an evening class, now is the time to mention it. You can also mention here any post-experience that is relevant, eg a holiday job.

— Put dashes where questions do not apply in order to show that you haven't missed them.

— Finally, check that you've signed the form.

— Keep a copy just as you do with your letters. (Libraries, post offices, stations and some shops often have photocopying machines.)

Sometimes you are asked to fill in an application form on the spot when you go for an interview. Be prepared for this and take with you the same sort of checklist that we recommend above for telephone applications. The employer will not think any less of you if you are able to fill in the facts accurately and quickly because you have already written them down. It is very difficult to remember dates and numbers on the spot, and it also looks bad if you cannot remember how to spell something.

Curriculum vitae

WHAT IT IS

This is an account of your own history in the form of a list. You include schools, exams, employment (if any) and some personal details (see the examples on pages 142 and 143).

WHY YOU MAY NEED ONE

Some employers ask for a cv (as they are usually called) to be enclosed with your application. You can also use it whenever

```
MARK GARY BROWN
32 PARK AVENUE, MANCHESTER M30 5BQ
Tel: 061-246 8093


DATE OF BIRTH: ..........    AGE NOW: ..........

SCHOOLS ATTENDED:
     (Name & town)                 (From)            (To)

COLLEGES ATTENDED:
     (Name & town)                 (From)            (To)

QUALIFICATIONS:
     (Name of exam & examining board) (Subject) (Grade)

     (Include all school/college examinations
     which you have passed.)

CERTIFICATES & OTHER QUALIFICATIONS:
     (Name of exam & examining board   (Subject)   (Grade)

     (Include any other qualifications/certificates you
     have which you think would be relevant or of
     interest to employers, eg sports certificates,
     music and drama exams etc.)

POSITIONS HELD:
     (eg class representative, sports captain,
     membership of a sports team, library assistant,
     school choir etc.)

INTERESTS AND ACTIVITIES:
     (List your hobbies, not too many but enough to
     show something of your personality and particularly
     things that are relevant that demonstrate responsibility,
     experience, fitness, eg if you are applying for
     a job involving technical skills you might say you
     enjoy motorbike maintainance or if the job involves
     handling money you might have experience of handling
     funds at school or clubs or for charity.)

FURTHER EDUCATIONAL PLANS:
     (Name of course & college)
     (Dates & times of classes)     (Qualifications if any)

     (You can include day and evening classes, full or
     part-time, which you are already attending or
     would like to to study (explain which), eg typing,
     languages, technical skills, additional GCEs and
     CSEs.)

EXPERIENCE:
     (Only use this heading if you have had any holiday
     or evening jobs including amateur, voluntary and
     unpaid work.  It is useful to list these to show
     that you have some idea of the working world.)

REFERENCES:
     (Name of referee)     (Address)          (Tel no)
(1)
(2)
(3)
```

Sample layout for a curriculum vitae for a first job

*NB. Never put a heading if you have nothing to list under it!
Leave it out altogether.*

```
SUSAN CAROLINE SMITH
11 BOLTON STREET, BRISTOL SHQ E10
Tel:  BRISTOL 59178

DATE OF BIRTH: ..........

AGE NOW: ..........

MARRIED/SINGLE

EDUCATION:
         (Name of schools/colleges & towns)          (From) - (To)
         (List schools, colleges, university including
         institutions where you have studied part-time.)

QUALIFICATIONS:
         (Number & names of exams)        (Subjects)

         Group school exams together, eg
         4 Oxford GCE O levels: English, Biology, Maths, Geography
         List any subsequent examinations separately.)

PREVIOUS EMPLOYMENT:
         (Name of company/employer & town) (Position) (From) - (To)
         (Brief description of responsibilities.)

OTHER ACTIVITIES:
         (It is best to list only specific positions or
         achievements or one or two sports or club memberships
         which are important to you or relevant. But it is
         useful to list anything that indicates qualities such
         as leadership or responsibility, eg youth leader.)

OTHER QUALIFICATIONS:
         (If you can speak or write any other language do say
         so.  It isn't always clear from the list of qualific-
         ations.  Such an ability can be an advantage in many
         different jobs, even when the connection is not obvious.
         Also mention driving licence, secretarial skills,
         computing and work processing ability.)

REFERENCES:
         (NAME)          (COMPANY)                (POSITION)
     (1)
     (2)
     (3)
```

Sample curriculum vitae for those changing jobs
Again, do not include any headings where you have nothing to list.

you want to enclose full details with one of your own letters (for example, see the sample on-spec letter on page 132 where it says 'I enclose details of my education and particular interests').

If you send a cv you won't have to give too much detail in your covering letter. As we said earlier, a short uncluttered letter with only essential details is always best. Take pity on the poor employer who has to read the life history of every applicant just to find out who they are and what job they are applying for.

However, you can use your covering letter to emphasise any points in your cv which you think are particularly relevant, eg qualifications for the job or appropriate experience in a holiday job.

It is essential that a curriculum vitae is laid out as neatly as possible. Ideally it should be typed — otherwise printed clearly. Keep a number of copies (photocopies are convenient and acceptable) ready to send out.

Make sure all the details are as accurate and as full as possible. As with application forms, be entirely honest.

On the following pages we show ways of setting out a curriculum vitae. It should be slightly different according to whether you are a school-leaver or have already had a job. If you need more than one page to write your cv use a second sheet — not the back of the first one.

Rembember that no CV should be longer than two pages.

Chapter 6

THE INTERVIEW

When you are asked to go for an interview you will probably feel nervous and anxious. What do I do? What do I say? Will I get the job? Instead of fretting over questions like that, try to see it from the employer's point of view. He has asked this unknown person to come along for an interview. What will he expect to see? What does he *want* to see?

Whatever the job he will want to see someone

- who looks pleasant
- who looks clean and tidy
- who looks cheerful and enthusiastic
- who seems to want the job
- who knows which job they have applied for and why they want it.

He is going to assume that you have come along because you want the job, so you must be prepared to say *why* you are applying for the job and what makes you think you will be good at it. It is important to sound enthusiastic, even if the job doesn't sound all that interesting. Remember that the job is interesting to *him*, so you had better be interested too.

Aim to make a good impression right from the start when you walk into his office, so

☐ Be on time, allowing plenty of time for traffic jams, trains being late etc. Most people hate to be kept waiting and it will annoy the interviewer from the start if you are even ten minutes late.

☐ Have an early night beforehand, so that you are not tired and jaded.

☐ Dress respectably. There's no need to get all dressed up but make sure you look clean and tidy. Scruffy jeans, dirty hair and hands, scuffed plimsolls won't impress him.

☐ Speak in a firm, confident voice. Don't mumble so that the interviewer has trouble making out what you are saying.

☐ Don't sit down or light up a cigarette until asked.

☐ Look the interviewer in the eye.

How the interview is planned

First, take a deep breath outside. The impression you make on entering will be the most important so put all you can into it. Smile and be ready to shake hands. Look interested and alert. If you enter appearing confident, it will help you throughout the interview.

1. *He will start* by trying to put you at your ease, chatting about the weather, asking if you smoke etc. Sit down and relax, but don't overdo it! It's all right to light up, but don't chain-smoke or drop ash all over the carpet. Keep looking at him and try to look pleasant and *interested*. (Think how depressing it must be to interview someone who stares gloomily at the carpet and doesn't show any enthusiasm at all for the job.)

2. *He'll try to get you talking* by asking about what you have been doing since you left school and what you have been doing generally for the last few years. He wants you to talk, but beware of rambling on for too long. He is trying to get a picture of your likes and dislikes, what you are good at and bad at, and so build up a picture of your whole personality. Answer honestly, but don't be negative and talk about what you *can't* do unless you are specifically asked that question. Try not to be boastful either. Even if you have very unusual qualifications or did very well at school, be careful how you talk about it or you will be written off as big-headed. It is also important not to make snide or unpleasant remarks about any previous employer.

3. *He'll go on to the application form or letter* and ask you to fill in the details of what you did at school and what you have been doing since. Be patient and answer fully, even if it is all there already on the application form. Avoid giving 'yes' and 'no' answers. He might ask how you would like to see your career developing, so try to think out what you would like to be doing in five years' time. He's trying to find out if you have *thought* about the future. He's also trying to find out what is important to you — money, status etc.

4. *He'll now try to find out why you applied for this job.* You may have picked it with a pin out of the evening paper, but it's not tactful to say so. You must think of reasons why you applied for the job and what makes you think you are suitable for it. You can link up here with what you found out about yourself in Chapter 1 in the self-analysis section. For instance, you can say you are applying for a job in an old folks' home because you like being with other people and have already helped out at a local institution in your spare time; you have lots of patience and don't get easily upset by other people's tantrums. In other words you have to *sell yourself* for the job.

Above all, you must sound really keen, as if you actually *want* the job — a surprising number of people fail in interviews because they sound as if they couldn't care less about the job.

He will also want to find out if you have really thought about the job and what it entails. You must sound enthusiastic and confident about your ability to do the job, but at the same time show that you are aware of the problems. For example, if you are applying for a job as a dental nurse it's as well to show that you are aware that it's a tiring job, but you can mention that your general health has always been good and you would hate to have a job where you were sitting down all day etc.

5. *He'll try to find out what sort of person you are.* At this point he might ask about your hobbies and outside interests. Be honest here. Don't make up stories about this for the sake of something to say — the interviewer might

turn out to be an enthusiastic birdwatcher or stamp-collector too, and then you'll be caught out.

6. *He'll try to unearth any future problems* by asking about your family background. He might ask if you would be prepared to travel in the course of your work, or if you would be prepared to move to another town if the job took you there. Again, you should think about this beforehand and have an answer ready. He'll ask about your general health, especially if you are in a job that entails long hours and a lot of standing, to make sure you are up to the physical requirements of the job.

Checklist of key questions you will be asked

These are questions all interviewers ask, so make sure you have answers prepared.

- ☐ Tell me briefly what you have been doing over the last two to three years.
- ☐ When did you first decide to go for a career in . . . ?
- ☐ What made you apply for this job?
- ☐ What particularly attracts you about this job?
- ☐ What aspects of the job do you think you might find difficult?
- ☐ How would you like your career to develop/what would you like to be doing in five years' time?
- ☐ What do you particularly like doing in your spare time?
- ☐ Tell me about your family. What do your parents feel about your plans?
  And, if you already have (or had) a job . . .
- ☐ Why do/did you want to leave the job you have/had?

Your chance to learn about the job

The interview is also your chance to find out about the company and the job on offer. Many people forget this. It should be a two-way process where you learn about each other. Your turn will usually come at the end of the interview. Providing all has gone reasonably well the interviewer will ask if you have any questions. Don't be afraid to speak up at this point.

The sort of things that you should know by now about the job are the hours of work, the pay, holidays, training, promotion and the other employees. If you are not clear about any of these, ask. Don't make it appear like an interrogation. Be polite.

Checklist of key questions you ought to ask

- [ ] What are the normal working hours?
- [ ] How much will I earn?
- [ ] Do you have regular salary reviews?
- [ ] How much paid holiday would I be entitled to?
- [ ] Do you give any special training for the job?
- [ ] Do you have day-release schemes?
- [ ] Would there be any possibility of promotion?
- [ ] Would I be required to travel at all?
- [ ] Would I always be working at this branch?
- [ ] Who would I be working with?
- [ ] Who would I be responsible to?
- [ ] Is there any optional overtime work?
- [ ] Is there a pension scheme?
- [ ] Would I have to contribute to a pension scheme?

You might also ask if it is possible to see where you would be working if you haven't already been shown.

Telephone interviews

There is an increasing trend towards telephone interviewing. The employer does his preliminary interview over the telephone and then, if he likes the sound of you (quite literally) he will ask you to come along for a more formal interview. You may also find, having gone for a preliminary interview, that you are then rung up by the personnel officer for a background chat. In either event, it is most important that you should be well prepared. Always remember:

- [ ] Write out all the relevant details about yourself on a piece of paper in case you become flustered and suddenly cannot even remember the name of your school. It's reassuring to have a piece of paper in your hand with all that you need to say.

☐ Try to speak in a firm, clear voice. Don't mumble and 'um' and 'er' and say 'sort of' or 'you know' every other word. Your voice is the only thing the employer has to go on, so you must try to sound pleasant, self-assured (even if your knees are knocking) and capable.

☐ Come straight to the point and don't dither. 'I'm ringing about the advertisement in today's paper. It sounds very interesting. Could you tell me more about it please?'

☐ If you are ringing from a call-box, make sure you have an ample supply of coins — you don't want to be cut off in mid-sentence.

Conclusion

Remember that it is not the end of the world if they don't seem to like you, or if they say, 'Don't ring us. We'll ring you.' Look on it as good experience — after all, the more interviews you go to, the better you will become at them. Try to be objective and analyse what went wrong and then perhaps you won't make the same mistake next time.

Chapter 7

ACCEPTANCE

Letters of acceptance or refusal

If you receive an offer consider it and reply immediately. If the offer is made by telephone it is acceptable to ask if you can call back shortly. You may need a minute or so to consider, or to consult someone.

The employer will need to have your decision, one way or the other, quickly. It is just as important to refuse promptly so as not to waste any of his time. If the offer is made by letter you should reply in writing though the employer may ask you to telephone as well. Your letter should be straightforward and acknowledge the points in the letter offering you the job.

Sample letters for accepting or refusing are set out on pages 152 and 153.

Contract of employment

A contract of employment exists as soon as someone offers you a job at a certain rate of pay and you accept. A contract of employment is required by law. It is normally written, in the form of a letter, document or booklet, but it *can* be verbal.

In any case, the employer has to give you written particulars of your terms of employment within 13 weeks after starting work. The details cover:

- ☐ job title
- ☐ date of beginning the job
- ☐ pay

(Your address)

(Date)

(Name of person)
(Firm's name and address)

Dear (Name of person offering you job),

Thank you for your letter of .... (date)
offering me an appointment/job/position as
.... (title/description of job) with
.... (name of company). I am very
pleased to accept this offer. I note the points
set out in your letter.

I look forward to joining the company beginning
on .... (date) at .... (time).

Yours sincerely,

(Your signature)

(Your name printed clearly
underneath signature)

Sample letter accepting an offer of a job

(Your address)

(Date)

(Name of person)
(Firm's name and address)

Dear (Name of person offering you the job),

Thank you for your letter of .... (date)
offering me an appointment/job/position as
.... (name/description of job) with
.... (name of company). I much
appreciate this offer. I shall have to decline,
however, as (Reason - eg 'I have already accepted
another offer which I was awaiting when I came to
you for interview.' Give a polite reason if you
think you may one day want to work for this
company, otherwise do not expand at all).

Thank you for considering me.

Yours sincerely,

(Your signature)

(Your name printed clearly
underneath signature)

Sample letter declining an offer of a job

- [ ] when pay is made (weekly, monthly, etc)
- [ ] hours of work
- [ ] holiday entitlement and pay
- [ ] length of notice
- [ ] disciplinary and grievance procedures
- [ ] pension and sick pay entitlement (if any)
- [ ] any requirement to join a specific trade union.

If you are not given these written particulars once the 13 weeks are up, you should ask for them.

But you should make sure, *when you agree to take a job,* that you at least fully understand what the job is, what your hours and rate of pay are and what the holiday entitlement is. If you have any doubts or queries, clear them up at the beginning. It is no defence later to say that you didn't realise the job involved such long hours, or that you thought you were due four weeks' holiday when it turns out to be only two.

The contract of employment is a legal document — keep it. It is a form of protection for both you and the employer. Make sure you read it and any booklets or other literature that comes with it so that you know what you are letting yourself in for.

How to start

APPEARANCES

Make a good impression and play safe just as you did at the interview. You succeeded at the interview but you will still be on trial at first. Make sure of the time you are supposed to arrive. Allow plenty of time to get there and arrive a little early. Dress appropriately for the work and always appear clean, neat and organised. You will feel better if you start off on the right foot. Appearances always matter and until they know you and your work your employers can only judge by what they see. It is important to appear willing and interested.

Whatever you do don't be big-headed. Feel pleased with yourself for getting the job and/or your exams by all means, but be quiet about this at the office. Whatever your achievements, you are only a beginner at the job and have to learn first. Everybody else is more experienced.

LEARNING

In larger firms there may be an established procedure where you are shown the building, introduced to your colleagues and given useful information and an introduction to the job. In some companies it may be more informal. If you find that you are left to get on and are not clear what you have to do or where to find something, do not be afraid to ask. It is much better to ask than to waste time doing nothing or doing something wrong.

What you are told in the first days and weeks will seem a lot to take in but you will be surprised at how different you feel at the end of the first month. You will absorb most things without realising. It is important to make a special effort if you find something difficult.

OTHER PEOPLE

Be friendly to everyone but it is wise to develop friendships slowly. It can be hard to judge people when you first meet them especially when there are a number of new faces all at once. Take advice from those to whom you are responsible. It is safest to refer to them and not always to rely on the advice of others in the office. Sometimes petty jealousies or disputes can arise in offices and it is unwise to become involved until you know what you are doing.

You will probably be working closer to adults and associating with older people more than you have before. Some may be patronising, some may seem superior, but as you begin to feel more at home with your work you will be able to adjust to them.

WORK

Working in your first job will be completely different from anything else you have done. Even if you have had a holiday job (and are familiar with the eight-hour day, one-hour lunch break and coffee breaks) it will be different because now your job is permanent and you are earning your living.

Things you should know

While you are learning your job make a mental note to learn more about the conditions of your employment. You may not need to use the information immediately, but sooner or later one or more of the things listed below could become important to you. It's wise to know where you stand in advance.

The answers to the questions below may be set out clearly in a written contract or statement (see 'Contract of employment' above) but you may have to ask. In a big firm there will be a personnel department or a personnel manager whose job it is to explain these things. In a small firm the person who pays you should know the answer to most of these questions. Otherwise ask your immediate boss.

SICKNESS

Who should I notify? What are the requirements for medical certificates? What sick pay am I entitled to?

BONUSES AND INCENTIVES

Are there any?

GRIEVANCES

What is the procedure for expressing these?

NOTICE

How much notice must I give my employer? How much notice must he give me if he wants to terminate my employment?

DISMISSAL/REDUNDANCY

What is the company policy regarding compensation?

DISCIPLINARY RULES AND PROCEDURES

What are they? Are they listed anywhere?

TRADE UNIONS

Which ones operate in this company? How active are they?
Who is the union representative?

Chapter 8

WHILE YOU WAIT

You have followed all the advice in this book, applied for every job you seemed to be even remotely suited for, and still you have not found a job. Now what do you do?

Most important, don't despair. With high unemployment, lots of people must be in your position. There is nothing personal about it. Here is what you do now.

Plan of action

1. Try to find out if you are doing anything wrong or could do any more. If you have applied for lots of jobs and never got so far as an interview, either you are applying for the wrong jobs or you are failing to apply properly. Read over Chapter 1 again, and this time get a friend to answer the questions for you. The result might surprise you — people often have very misguided ideas about their personalities and their abilities. This is where you might find out that you have been applying for the *wrong kind* of jobs or have more alternatives than you imagine.

   Having straightened that out, have another think about *how* you are applying for jobs. Are you following the sample letters we laid out (see pp 135-138)? Is your handwriting terrible? Be prepared to be critical of yourself. Next time you write a letter of application, show it to a friend, or the careers officer, and ask if it is good enough. Are you filling in the application forms carefully and neatly, answering all the questions? It could be that your letters and forms are ending up in the wastepaper basket because you are not taking enough time and trouble with them.

2. Go and badger your careers officer and the employment adviser at the local Jobcentre. Tell them your problems and see what they can do for you. Don't be shy of asking for help as often as you like — remember, *it is their job to help you find a job*. See them regularly and do not give up.

3. Find something to do. Not having a job can be very demoralising and you soon get out of the habit of working. Hanging round street corners isn't going to get you anywhere. Try to keep mentally alert and up to date; don't just drift.

   There are some part-time jobs around — look in the local papers. Some employment agencies specialise in part-time and temporary staff for offices. etc. Look in the Yellow Pages under 'Employment Agencies'. It is wise to check the effect of part-time work on your entitlement to unemployment benefit. Also consider unpaid work for organised charities and volunteer groups or for friends or family. They may not be the kind of job you had in mind, but it is better than nothing. Employers will be impressed by your initiative if you have found something to do, even if it is only street-sweeping. And who knows, it might lead to a full-time job or to meeting people who know of one.

   But remember, don't take on anything that will hinder your hunt for a full-time job. You must be able to go to interviews if asked. Beware of night-time jobs in bars and discos that will make you bleary-eyed and yawning when you turn up for a 9 am interview. Beware, too, of taking on a temporary job where there is a legal or moral obligation to give a long period of notice: it might cost you your new job. Make it clear from the start that you are looking for a full-time job.

4. Improve your qualifications or lower your sights. With 50 or 60 applicants for a job, employers can afford to pick and choose, and naturally they choose the people with the best qualifications. If you are having no luck in your job-hunting, or if you are in a dead-end job with no prospects, it could be lack of suitable qualifications that is holding you back. You have three options:

   (a) you can go back to full-time education to get the necessary O levels, or whatever;

(b) you can lower your sights, start further down the ladder and improve your qualifications through day-release or evening classes (see Chapter 3 where we give details of courses available); *or*

(c) you may be eligible to go on a Government training scheme, either through the Youth Training Scheme (YTS) or through the Job Training Scheme.

The Youth Training Scheme (YTS)

This is a scheme specially set up by the Manpower Services Commission, who also run the Jobcentres, to help young people who have been unable to find a job. They give you a chance to learn some basic skills and try out different kinds of work — office work, working with tools or machinery, working in a shop, and so on.

While on a scheme you gain real experience of work and working conditions, and it also gives you the chance to show people what you can do. The scheme can last for anything from two weeks to two years, but if you are offered a job while on a scheme you can start right away.

It aims to provide up to two years' high quality training and planned work expansion, with a certificate at the end of it.

Almost 400,000 places are provided by a network of over 4000 managing agents and 1500 sponsors. Two-thirds of YTS people move on into jobs or further full-time education or training, having gained the YTS Certificate.

An important feature of the scheme is the guarantee of an offer of a place by Christmas to all minimum age school leavers unemployed during the first year after leaving school.

PROGRAMMES

Training programmes are sponsored by a wide variety of organisations — employers, local authorities, voluntary organisations and training organisations. The majority of places are provided by employers.

Other programmes include: *Community Projects* (planned work experience with training and/or education). Can be in a workshop environment, on projects within the community or on placements with employers.

Training Workshops – give the opportunity to acquire practical experience and training in a range of skills. Types of training include metalwork, pottery, new technology, catering and office skills.

Information Technology Centres
These offer basic training in micro-computing, electronics and word processing, and work experience in development and manufacture of products based on new technology. They are usually run by local authorities or private sponsors.

PAYMENT

Employees receive a normal wage and pay tax and National Insurance contributions as normal. Trainees (in the other programmes) get a weekly allowance of £27.30 in the first year and £35 in the second year.

Applications for training courses run by the MSC can be made through Jobcentres or your local Careers Office.

Community Programme

Provides temporary jobs for long-term unemployed adults. This improves chances of finding jobs by providing, for example, a recent reference from an employer.

Recruitment is normally limited to those aged 18-24 who have been unemployed for six months or more during the last nine months and 25 and over who have been unemployed for at least 12 months in the last 15.

The project is usually limited to 52 weeks and workers are paid an hourly rate for the jobs.

Most projects have a mix of full-time and part-time employees. Most projects are sponsored by local authorities, voluntary organisations, nationalised industries etc.

Voluntary Projects Programme

The purpose is to provide unemployed people with constructive activity which will develop existing skills.

Projects should encourage unemployed people to do community work on an unpaid, voluntary basis.

Job Training Scheme

These courses are part of a Government-organised training scheme run by the MSC's Training Services Division and used to be known as the Training Opportunities Scheme or TOPS. The courses are vocational, ie they train people in skills which will enable them to move into a job straightaway. They are aimed particularly at people who for various reasons have had trouble in finding, or holding down, jobs.

ARE YOU ELIGIBLE?

To be accepted on a course, you have to satisfy certain conditions:

1. You must be 19 or over and must have been away from full-time education for two years.
2. You must intend to take up employment using the skill in which you will be training.
3. You must either be unemployed, or else willing to give up your present job in order to take the full-time training.
4. You have not taken a Government training course during the past three years. This condition may not apply if you want to take an advanced course in a subject you have already studied.
5. You must be suited to the course you choose. Trained staff will decide this, taking into account your previous experience, abilities and potential.

If you are disabled, some of these conditions may not apply.

HOW TO APPLY

There are Jobcentres or employment offices in most towns. Call in at one of these and ask for an appointment with an interviewing officer, or if this is not convenient for you, write or telephone. The address will be in the phone book and they are usually open Monday to Friday, 9 am to 5 pm.

There are many free leaflets giving further information on these courses. They can be obtained from any of the following Training Services Regional Offices:

LONDON

TSD Office for London, 166 High Holborn, London WC1V 7AT
01-836 1213

SCOTLAND

TSD Office for Scotland, 9 St Andrew Square, Edinburgh EH2 2QX
031-225 8500

NORTH WEST

TSD Office for the North West, Washington House, The Capital Centre, New Bailey Street, Manchester M3 5ER
061-833 0251

WALES

TSD Office for Wales, 4th floor, Companies House, Crown Way, Maindy, Cardiff CF4 3UT
0222 388588

SOUTH WEST

TSD Office for the South West, Bridge House, Sion Place, Clifton, Bristol BS8 4XA
0272 32231

SOUTH EAST

TSD Office for the South East, Telford House, Hamilton Close, Basingstoke, Hants
0256 29266

NORTHERN

TSD Office for the North, Derwent House, Washington Centre, Washington New Town, Tyne and Wear NE38 7ST
0632 466161

YORKS AND HUMBERSIDE

TSD Office for Yorks and Humberside, Jubilee House, 33-41 Park Place, Leeds LS1 2RL
0532 446299

MIDLANDS

TSD Office for the Midlands, Alpha Tower, Suffolk Street, Queensway, Birmingham B1 1TT
021-632 4144

The Job Finder's Book

ALLOWANCES

If you take a course, you will be paid a weekly allowance (which is higher than unemployment benefit rates) during your training. This allowance varies according to your family commitments and whether or not you train away from home. These payments will be revised at intervals so that they keep pace with inflation, so check at your local Jobcentre.

WHICH COURSE WILL YOU TAKE?

There are courses in over 500 subjects, from welding to shorthand typing; from bricklaying to systems analysis.

SKILLCENTRES

If you take a course in a basic craft skill, you will probably be taught at a Skillcentre. These centres are equipped with the latest machinery and equipment and are designed to resemble ordinary working conditions.

OTHER TOPS COURSES

Apart from courses in Skillcentres, you can take a course in a variety of subjects at certain colleges and training centres. Subjects covered include hotel and catering, office and commercial skills, preparatory courses, and technician training.

PREPARATORY COURSES

These are intended for people whose reading, writing and arithmetic falls short of the standard necessary either to get a job or to pass a pre-entry test for a course at a higher level. Taking a preparatory course won't prevent you from being eligible to take another course; in fact it can be a substitute for the pre-entry test. Preparatory courses are available at many local colleges.

SHORT INDUSTRIAL TRAINING COURSES

Again, if you take one of these courses you will still be able to take a full Job Training Scheme course. They are ideal for the person who is not sure what he or she wants to do and does not want to be committed to a long period of training; they all last less than 13 weeks. These short industrial courses are intended to introduce you to a specific skill in some area of industry or commerce, but remember that they will vary from area to area.